Calling All Catholics

GAYLE,

I HOPE THE BOOK WILL HELP STRENGTHEN YOUR FAITH! MAY HE GUIDE YOU IN ALL TRUTH!

LOVE YOU,

[illegible]

Calling All Catholics

A Message from the Word of God

Mark Aldridge

TATE PUBLISHING & *Enterprises*

Published by Tate Publishing & Enterprises, LLC
127 E. Trade Center Terrace | Mustang, Oklahoma 73064 USA
1.888.361.9473 | www.tatepublishing.com

Tate Publishing is committed to excellence in the publishing industry. The company reflects the philosophy established by the founders, based on Psalm 68:11,
"The Lord gave the word and great was the company of those who published it."

Cover design by Lance Waldrop
Interior design by Jeff Fisher

Published in the United States of America

ISBN: 978-1-60799-942-3
1. Religion, Christian Theology, Apologetics
09.09.08

Acknowledgements

I would like to thank the LORD Jesus Christ for calling me and guiding me in this work for his glory and honor. I would also like to thank my grandmother for having modeled Christ through her abounding love, hospitality and countless prayers. I thank my wife and children for their patience while I was working on the book. I give a special thanks to Will Clark, Ken Harmon, Rob Myers, Matt Sheranko, and pastor Brain Shepard for their help with editing and for their encouragement.

Finally, I thank Tate Publishing for co-laboring in this work.

Introduction

The reason I decided to compare the Catechism of the Catholic Church to the Bible was to allow the reader an opportunity where by they could assess the texts simultaneously and formulate their own beliefs. Our beliefs or convictions must have a foundation upon which we can trust and know that they have merit. It is my conviction that many people are placing their trust in ideas or traditions that simply don't have merit. In God's economy there is a standard that is sure and unchanging. He desires our feet to be firmly placed upon the Rock, which is the unchanging Word of God. That Rock is not moved by public opinion or by what man supposes to be true. The reader will have a unique opportunity to review the two writings and, in the end, will be able to render an individual verdict. It is my hope and prayer that, as you review the writings, you ask the LORD to guide you in all truth. I was married in 1998 to my beloved wife, Gretchen. Prior to our getting married, I had just gotten back from Calvary Chapel Bible College, where I was seeking the LORD's direction and the call to missions he had placed on my life. Upon returning to Maryland, I had not found a church home. My wife was raised Catholic, and I had been raised in the Baptist church. Although we had been raised in two different churches, we professed the same faith in the LORD Jesus Christ. So, we had to decide where we would be married, and Gretchen wanted to be married in the church where she was raised. We proceeded to make wedding plans to be married in the Catholic Church. After we were married, I knew we had to find a church we could agree on. I was not familiar with Catholic doctrine until we had our first child. It wasn't until then that I realized how important it was for a Catholic to have their child baptized as an infant and that Catholic's believe this is a means of salvation. I, on the other hand, did not see this lining up with the Word of God. So, it was then that I decided to get a copy of the catechism of the Catholic Church, published April 1995. It did not take me very long to discover that the truths I held dear and to be foundational to the faith were quite different than those found in the catechism. It is my hope and prayer that through this earnest work of comparison, God will be glorified and that those who profess to be Christians would embrace the word of God rather than the traditions of men.

Second Timothy 4:1–5 says,

> I charge you therefore before God and the LORD Jesus Christ, who will judge the living and the dead at his appearing and His kingdom: preach the word! Be ready in season and out of season. Convince, rebuke, exhort, with all longsuffering and teaching. For the time will come when they will not endure sound doctrine, but according to their own desires, because they have itching ears, they will heap up for themselves teachers;. But you be watchful in all things, endure afflictions, do the work of an evangelist, fulfill your ministry.[1]

As you read the comparison, you will note that I do not comment on every paragraph and I simply skip some paragraphs for the sake of avoiding redundant discussion.

Calling all Catholics

†

A catechism should faithfully and systematically present the teaching of Sacred Scripture, the living Tradition in the Church and the authentic Magisterium, as well as the spiritual heritage of the Fathers, Doctors, and saints of the Church, to allow for a better knowledge of the Christian mystery and for enlivening the faith of the People of God.

Page 4, section 2

Hebrews 4:12 says, "For the word of God is living and active, sharper than any two edged sword, piercing even to the division of soul and spirit, and of joints and marrow, and a discerner of the thoughts and intents of the heart." Although, the Bible does refer to itself as living, you will not find any reference for any such, "living tradition." In fact, most references to tradition are negative. Let's look at some of them. Acts 14:15 says,

> And saying, "Men, why are you doing these things? We also are men with the nature as you, and preach to you that you should turn from these vain things to the living God, who made the heaven, the earth, the sea, and all things that are in them."

The context in the book of Acts reveals that Paul and Barnabas were very upset because the people were getting ready to offer worship to them, and they rebuke them, saying, "Turn to the living God." First Peter 1:18 says, "Knowing that you were not redeemed from your aimless conduct received by tradition from your fathers." It is important to note that traditions have no redeeming power, and this verse makes that clear. In Titus 1:14, Paul writes, "Not giving heed to Jewish fables and commandments of men." Paul writes to the church in Colossi,

> Beware lest anyone cheat you through philosophy and empty deceit, according to the tradition of men, according to the basic principles of the world, and not according to Christ. For in Him dwells all the fullness of the Godhead bodily; and you are complete in him, who is the head of all principality and power.
>
> Colossians 2:8–9 (NKJV)

Here, I think it's important to note the LORD's choice of words. He says, "Beware lest anyone cheat you through empty deceit..." I believe he is saying it would be a shame to have a belief system with various rituals and practices which have no merit or spiritual value in his economy. Furthermore, how tragic it would be to invest your life in this belief system and come to find out that the very things you thought were spiritual in nature have no eternal value with God. It is my belief that many professing Christians are caught up in practices that simply can't be found in the Word of God.

†

Grace, the fruit of the sacraments, is the irreplaceable condition for Christian living, just as participation in the Church's Liturgy requires faith.

page 5, section 2

"Just as participation in the Church's Liturgy requires faith." Here you find, "grace, the fruit of the sacraments, is the irreplaceable condition for Christian living." It would seem as though they are suggesting that grace has something to do with sacraments. This is extremely problematic for the authors because grace, by definition, is, "divine love and protection given to mankind by God or a virtue granted by God" (Merriam-Webster Dictionary) Grace has nothing to do with an action on our part or the church's part. Here, it seems to be an interchanging of words. You will not find the fruit of the sacraments found in God's Word. But you will find the fruit of the Spirit, meaning one has been born of the spirit of God or accepted Christ into their hearts. In Gal 5:22–24, Paul writes, "But the fruit of the Spirit is love, joy, peace, longsuffering, kindness, goodness, gentleness, self-control. Against such there is no law. And those who are Christ's have crucified the flesh with it's passions and desires. If we live in the Spirit, let us also walk in the Spirit." So, to sum up this section, I would say they have erred in what they deem irreplaceable. The Spirit of God is what is irreplaceable for Christian living, not the fruit of the sacraments.

†

Christ is always present in his Church, especially in the sacraments.

page 5, section 2

First of all, we must establish what the church is. The church is made up of people who have accepted Jesus as their savior and believe in what his word teaches. The church is not subject to a building, hierarchy, or any sect of people. The church is broad and changes from town to town or country to country, but what does not change in the church is the central belief that Jesus alone became the propitiation for our sins and the central belief in his unchanging word. The author of Heb 1:3 writes, "Who being the righteousness of His glory and the express image of His person, and upholding all things by the word of His power, when He had by Himself purged our sins, sat down at the right hand of the majesty on high." John writes in his epistle, 1 John 2:2, "And He Himself is the propitiation for our sins and not for ours only but also for the whole world." In 1 John 4:10–13 he writes,

> In this is love, not that we loved God, but that he loved us and sent His Son to be the propitiation for our sins. Beloved, if God so loved us, we also ought to love one another. No one has seen God at any time. If we love one another, God abides in us, and His love has been perfected in us. By this we know that we abide in Him and He in us, because He has given us of His Spirit.
>
> 1 John 4:10–13 (NKJV)

We should note that as believers in Christ and his finished work on the cross, we have his Spirit in us (Rom 8:9). So, it would go without needing to be said that Christ is always present in his church or people who comprise the church. Furthermore, if Christ has placed his spirit in the believer (and he has), I don't know why the authors say, "especially in the sacrament." Christ lives and moves in his people, not in a Christian rite. Not to say that Christ does not bless these rites, because He does. But, by reading this sentence one might think Christ is the baptismal water, when in fact, Christ is in the person accepting Christ not in the water. Jesus rose bodily and sent his Spirit, and those who are born of his Spirit are changed by his Spirit, not by a Christian rite or any other physical act.

†

The Catechism of the Catholic Church, which I approved June 25th last and the publication of which I today order by virtue of my Apostolic Authority, is a statement of the Church's faith and of Catholic doctrine, attested to or illumined by Sacred Scripture, the Apostolic Tradition, and the Church's magisterium.

page 5, section 3

I would like to take a look at this statement's first sentence. I am all for statements being attested to or illumined by sacred Scripture. But, this is where this sentence should end. The only standard by which men and women will be judged is the Word of God. The apostolic traditions and the church's magisterium change. You know, Jesus had a lot to say about the traditions of men, or as it was at that time, the traditions of the religious ruling class. Let's take a look at the Gospel of Mark and see what Jesus has to say about traditions of men. Mark 7:4–13 says,

> When they come from the marketplace, they do not eat unless they wash. And there are many other things which they have received and hold, like the washing of cups, pitchers, copper vessels, and couches. Then the Pharisees and scribes asked Him, "Why do your disciples not walk according to the tradition of the elders, but eat bread with unwashed hands?" He answered and said to them, "Well did Isaiah prophesy of you hypocrites, as it is written: 'This people honors Me with their lips, But their heart is far from Me. And in vain they worship Me, Teaching as doctrines the commandments of men.' For laying aside the commandment of God, you hold the tradition of men—the washing of pitchers and cups, and many other such things you do." He said to them, "All too well you reject the commandment of God, that you may keep your tradition. For Moses said, 'Honor your father and your mother'; and, 'He who curses father or mother, let him be put to death.' But you say, 'If a man says to his father or mother, "Whatever profit you might have received from me is Corban"'—(that is, a gift to God), then you no longer let him do anything for his father or his mother, making the word of God of no effect through your tradition which you have handed down. And many such things you do."
>
> Mark 7:3–13 (NKJV)

There are a few things in these verses that I believe are central to the gospel message and the LORD's heart. He says in verse six quoting (Isaiah 29:13), "This people honors me with their lips, but their heart is far from me." Here, the LORD is exposing the sinful nature of the heart and the need for it to be converted. You see, the Pharisees knew more about the law and rituals than any of the other people, yet their hearts had not been converted. They were trusting in their birthright as Pharisees and their religious practices, which have no power to convert the heart or soul. The sad reality for the Pharisee, or anyone else who has not been born of the Spirit, is that they are worshiping God in vain. Mark 7:7 says, "And in vain they worship me, teaching as doctrines the commandments of men." . People teach as doctrines the commandments of men rather than the Word of God, this keeps their hearts from being converted, and their worship of God is in vain. The sad reality of these verses is that they are still very present in many churches today.

†

At the conclusion of this document presenting the Catechism of the Catholic Church, I beseech the Blessed Virgin Mary, mother of the Incarnate Word and Mother of the Church, to support with her powerful intercession the catechetical work of the entire Church on every level, at this time when she is called to a new effort of evangelization. May the light of the true faith free humanity from the ignorance and slavery of sin in order to lead it to the only freedom worthy of the name (cf. Jn 8:32*) that of life in Jesus Christ under the guidance of the Holy Spirit, here below and in the kingdom of heaven, in the fullness if the blessed vision of God face to face (Cor* 13:12;2 *Cor* 5:6–8*).*

page 6, section 3

Here the authors refer to Mary, the earthly mother of Jesus, as the "Mother of the Church" and call on her for powerful intercession. They also say she is called to a new effort of evangelization. I think it is important for us to have a biblical understanding of just who Mary is and was in her ministry. First, who is Mary? She is a sinner who is saved by the grace of God. Granted, she was a righteous young women, otherwise God would not have chosen her to be the earthly mother of Jesus. But, she is like you and me and every other human being who was born with sin and was in need of a savior. Second, she was not sinless, or else Jesus would not have had to have come in the flesh because we would already have had the first sinless human being, Mary. Romans 3:23 illustrates this point quite clearly as Paul writes, "For all have sinned and fall short of the glory of God." If Mary and Jesus were both sinless, then you would have to rewrite this verse and the Bible. This verse might read something like this, "All have sinned, except Mary and Jesus and fall short of the glory God." Third, what new effort of evangelization is there? Evangelization is the same today as it always has been, leading people to faith in the living God. Lastly, the sentence that starts out, "May the light of the true faith," is troubling. This statement is troubling because it is exclusive and would seem to be implying that non-Catholics are not a part of the true faith. Although, I would propose that any faith not founded and rooted in the Word of God will quickly find itself outside of the true faith which is found in the Word of God.

†

Its principal sources are the Sacred Scriptures, the Fathers of the Church, the liturgy, and the Church's magisterium

page 11, section 11

This sentence should end after the first comma. Any time you start to add to the Sacred Scriptures, you find yourself in a compromising position. You see, either the Bible is the word of God, or it is not. If the Bible is not our sole source of truth, then we have no basis of truth. We would simply be making things up as we have gone through time. I don't know about you, but I'm not about to risk my eternal future based on what a man or groups of men have told me to be true. No, I want to base my eternal future on something that is tried and true. John 1:1 says, "In the beginning was the Word, and the Word was with God, and the Word was God." John 1:14 says, "And the Word became flesh and dwelt among us, and we beheld His glory, the glory as of the only begotten of the Father, full of grace and truth." I want to take a moment to look at John 1:1 because I believe upon this verse the whole Christian faith either rises or falls. You see, if the Word was with God in the beginning, then the Word is the standard upon which we will be judged eternally. John 1:14 goes on to say that the Word or Jesus also became flesh and dwelt among us. Hebrews 4:12–13 says,

> For the word of God is living and powerful, and sharper than any two-edged sword, piercing even to the division of soul and spirit, and of joints and marrow, and is a discerner of the thoughts and intents of the heart. And there is no creature hidden from His sight, but all things are naked and open to the eyes of Him to whom we must give account.

Here once again, you can see that the standard by which we will be judged or have to give an account is based solely on the Word of God. Lastly, Psalm 96:13 says, "For He is coming, for He is coming to judge the earth. God is coming to judge us, His standard for judgment is His truth and His truth is His word and the word became flesh." Psalm 119:160 says, "The entirety of your word is truth, and every one of your righteous judgments endures forever." First John 2: 4–5 says, "He who says, 'I know Him,' and does not keep His commandments, is a liar, and the truth is not in him. But whoever keeps His word truly the love of God is perfected in him. By this we know that we are in Him." I believe this is a very insightful verse. The only thing that will matter is what we as believers have done with his word. Lastly, notice in John 1:1, that the Word of God and Jesus are the same thing. If you want to have true prospective of who Jesus is, you have to have an understanding of what is in his written Word because the Bible is God's revelation of himself to us.[2] [3]

Our holy mother, the Church, holds and teaches that God, the first principle and last end of all things, can be known with certainty from the created world by the natural light of human reason.

page 20, paragraph 36

The first part of this sentence is problematic because it states we have a holy mother. When referring to the church, you won't find any references in the Bible that refers to the church or any other person as being a holy mother to the believer. The only person who was without sin is Jesus. Furthermore, when referring to the church, the Bible says that the church is the bride of Christ or the believers in Christ. In Rev. 19:7–10, John writes,

> Let us be glad and rejoice and give Him glory, for the marriage of the Lamb has come, and His wife has made herself ready." and to her it was granted to be arrayed in fine linen, clean and bright, for the fine linen is the righteous acts of the saints. Then he said to me, "Write: Blessed are those who are called to the marriage supper of the Lamb." And he said to me, "These are the true sayings of God." And I fell at his feet to worship him. But he said to me, "See that you do not do that. I am your fellow servant, and of your brethren who have the testimony of Jesus worship God. For the testimony of Jesus is the spirit of prophecy.

There are three important points made in these four verses. One, you can see the church being referred to as Christ's wife or bride, not as holy mother. Two, you see the saints being arrayed in fine linen. The saints are those of us who have been born of the spirit of God; it's not a title given by man. A saint is anyone who has been sanctified and set apart by the blood of Jesus. Three, you see John fall down to worship the angel from which he received his revelation and, quickly, you see the angel rebuke him. Our worship should only be directed at Jesus, our Lord, not angels, people, or any other inanimate objects.

†

It pleased God, in his goodness and wisdom, to reveal Himself and to make know the mystery of His will. His will was that men should have access to the Father, through Christ, the Word made flesh, in the Holy Spirit, and thus become shares in the divine nature.

page 23, paragraph 51

I couldn't agree more with this statement. You get a tremendous amount of truth in the above statement. First, you can see that God's will is for men to have access to him. How do we gain access to him? Through Christ and Christ alone, "for there is one mediator between God and man, the man Christ Jesus." Second, you have the Word made flesh. This is a simple statement, yet it has a deeper spiritual meaning. The Word is the Bible, and if that is true, and it is, then why don't people get to know God's Word? Through studying God's Word you are gaining a true understanding of who God is. You see, without studying his Word, we may think we are drawing close to Jesus, when in fact, we may be involved in idolatry.

†

The divine plan of revelation is realized simultaneously "by deeds and words which are intrinsically bound up with each other" and shed light on each other.

page 24, paragraph 53

The divine plan of revelation is realized when a person realizes that apart from Jesus and his holy spirit being born in you, that you're wretched, miserable, poor, blind, and naked. Revelation 3:15–21 says,

> I know your works, that you are neither cold nor hot. I could wish you were cold or hot. So then, because you are lukewarm, and neither cold nor hot, I will spew you out of My mouth. Because you say, "I am rich, have become wealthy, and have need of nothing" and do not know that you are wretched, miserable, poor, blind, and naked. I counsel you to buy from Me gold refined in the fire, that you may be rich; and white garments, that you may be clothed, that the shame of your nakedness may not be revealed; anoint your eyes with eye salve, that you may see. As many as I love, I rebuke and chasten. Therefore be zealous and repent. Behold I stand at the door and knock. If anyone hears My voice and opens the door, I will come in to him and dine with him, and he with Me. To him who overcomes I will grant to sit with Me on My throne as I also overcame and sat down with My Father on His throne. He who has an ear, let him hear what the Spirit says to the churches.
>
> Revelation 3:15–21 (NKJV)

God's divine plan is quite simple. He desires that all men should come to a saving knowledge of his Son. But, salvation is not accomplished because of our deeds, for we are not saved by works lest anyone should boast. Paul counsels the Church of Galatia,

> Knowing that a man is not justified by the works of the law but by faith in Jesus Christ, even we have believed in Christ Jesus, that we might be justified by faith in Christ and not by the works of the law; for by the law no flesh shall be justified.
>
> Galatians 2:16 (NKJV)

✝

He prepares him to welcome by stages the supernatural revelation that is to culminate in the person and mission of the incarnate word, Jesus Christ.

page 24, paragraph 53

This last part of section 53 makes this statement, from which one might conclude that there are certain steps or stages to gaining God's supernatural revelation, a system if you will. The only system God prescribes that I'm aware of is to be born of his Spirit. Then we gain further understanding by faith, prayer, and diving into the Word of God. You will get all the supernatural revelation you need by practicing these disciplines. God promises to instruct us in all things pertaining to godliness by the Holy Spirit.

✝

God, who creates and conserves all things by his Word.

page 24, paragraph 54

I couldn't agree more with this statement. Once again, if this statement is true, then why aren't people eagerly searching his Word, by which all things are held together?

†

For he wishes to give eternal life to all those who seek salvation by patience in well doing.

page 25, paragraph 55

Here again, there seems to be some confusion as to how a person gets eternal life, and it has nothing to do with patience or well doing. Paul explains this truth in his letter to the church in Rome.

> Therefore by the deeds of the law no flesh will be justified in His sight, for by the law is the knowledge of sin. But now the righteousness of God apart from the law is revealed, being witnessed by the law and the prophets, even the righteousness of God which is through faith in Jesus Christ to all and on all who believe. For all have sinned and fall short of the glory of God, being justified freely by His grace through the redemption that is in Christ Jesus, whom God set forth to be a propitiation by His blood, through faith to demonstrate His righteousness, because in His forbearance God had passed over the sins that were previously committed, to demonstrate at the present time His righteousness, that He might be just and the justifier of the one who has faith in Jesus. Where is boasting then? It is excluded. By what law? Of works? No, but by the law of faith. Therefore we conclude that man is justified by faith apart from the deeds of the law. Or is He the God of the Jews only? Is he not also the God of the Gentile? Yes, of the Gentiles also, since there is one God who will justify the circumcised by faith and the uncircumcised through faith.
>
> Romans 3:20–30 (NKJV)

✝

Through the prophets, God forms his people in the hope of salvation, in the expectation of a new and everlasting covenant intended for all, to be written on their hearts. The prophets proclaim a radical redemption of the people of God, purification from all infidelities, a salvation which will include all the nations.

page 27, paragraph 64

The first part of the sentence is incorrect: "God forms His people in the hope of salvation." Remember, God is not willing that any should perish but that all should come to the saving knowledge of God (2 Peter 3:9). God used his prophets to tell of the one coming who would save them from their sins. God is still using people today, just like the prophets of old, to proclaim Jesus is the LORD and he alone provides radical redemption from sins and purification from all infidelities.

✝

The purest figure among them is Mary.

page 27, paragraph 64

Analyzing the last part of paragraph 64, we find that they list holy women of the Bible such as Sarah, Rebecca, Rachel, Miriam, Deborah, Hannah, Judith, and Esther. You need to be careful here not to put Mary or any of the other holy women, or men for that matter, mentioned in the Bible on some sort of pedestal. Romans 2:11 says, "For there is no respect of persons with God." God chooses to use these peoples' lives because they have faith in him. This is just another testimony of God's grace toward us. You must remember that Mary and every other believer throughout time were "the dust of the earth," and God chose to breathe life into them. You must also consider that God chose Mary to be the earthly mother of Jesus because she was a woman of faith who found favor in God's eyes. This does not mean she or any other man or woman of faith were without sin. Romans 3:23 says, "For all have sinned and fall short of the glory of God." This verse does not say, "all, expect Mary or any other person of faith."

†

Indeed, the apostolic preaching, which is expressed in a special way in the inspired books, was to be preserved in a continuous line of succession until the end of time.

page 30, paragraph 77

Paragraph 77 says, "Indeed, the apostolic preaching, which is expressed in a special way in the inspired books, was to be preserved in a continuous line of succession until the end of time." If this is true, I wonder why the Bible makes no mention of a continuous line of succession until the end of time. The implication of this is that there is a continuity of leadership in the church, as if it has its own priesthood that is continued. However, this is in conflict with what Hebrews teaches about the roll of Jesus as the final High Priest who has put an end to the function of the Levitical priesthood. His priesthood has a new covenant that is superior to the first and is realized completely in him. See Hebrews 8:1, 6–7 and 13. There is no mention of any association of this priesthood with men. In fact, this priesthood is vastly superior to the earthly priesthood because of who he is, where he is, and what he has done. But, the Bible does say, "Heaven and earth shall pass away, but My words will by no means pass away" (Matthew 24:35). Or, Isaiah 40:8 says, "The grass withers, the flower fades, but the word of our God stands forever." The LORD will preserve his word just as he has done from the beginning of time. The reason God chose to use believers to tell the world the good news of the gospel is because of his grace. You see, if we don't tell the redemption story, the very rocks would cry out.

†

This living transmission, accomplished in the Holy Spirit, is called Tradition, since it is distinct from Sacred Scripture, though closely connected to it.

page 30, paragraph 78

This supposed living transmission called Tradition is nowhere to be found in the Bible, just like the continuous line of succession. But, let's take a look at what the LORD has to say about tradition.

> Beware lest anyone cheat you through philosophy and empty deceit, according to the tradition of men, according to the basic principles of the world, and not according to Christ. For in Him dwells the fullness of the Godhead bodily; and you are complete in Him who is the head of all principality and power.
>
> Colossians 2:8–10

Please note two very important things in these verses: one, who Christ is, the Word that became flesh; and two, that you are already complete in him. We are not being made complete; we already are complete. It might seem like tradition is an active part of the Trinity or plays an equal role with the Holy Spirit. This simply is not true. In fact, these verses in Colossians are there to warn the reader about the empty deceit found in the traditions of men. Traditions will never complete us, only the Holy Spirit residing in us can accomplish this.

> Preach the word. Be ready in season and out of season. Convince, rebuke, exhort, with all longsuffering and teaching. For the time will come when they will not endure sound doctrine, but according to their own desires, because they have itching ears, they will heap up for themselves teachers; and they will turn their ears away from the truth and be turned aside to fables, but you be watchful in all things, endure afflictions, do the work of an evangelist, fulfill your ministry.
>
> 2 Timothy 4:2–5

Once again, you have to ask the question, "What is truth?" In John 14:6, Jesus said, "I'm the way, the truth, and the life no one comes to the Father except through Me." Psalm 138:2 says, "For you have magnified your word above all your name."

> Holding fast the faithful word as he has been taught, that he may be able, by sound doctrine, both to exhort and convict those who contradict. For there are many insubordinate, both idle talkers and deceivers, especially those of circumcision, whose

> mouths must be stopped, who subvert whole households, teaching things which they ought not for the sake of dishonest gain. One of them, a prophet of their own, said, "Cretans are always lairs, evil beasts, lazy glutton." This testimony is true. Therefore rebuke them sharply, that they may be sound in the faith, not giving heed to Jewish fables and commandments of men who turn from the truth.
>
> Titus 1:9–14

Here it is again: the truth. Who or what is the truth? God has already established that Jesus was the Word and the truth. Ref: John 1:1, "In the beginning was the Word, and the Word was with God, and the Word was God." If the teachings that are being taught are contrary with what is found in the Bible, then one must conclude that they are fables or the commandments of men.

> Then the scribes and Pharisees who were from Jerusalem came to Jesus, saying, "Why do your disciples transgress the tradition of the elder? For they do not wash their hands when they eat bread." But he answered and said to them, "Why do you also transgress the commandment of God because of your tradition? For God commanded saying, 'Honor your father and your mother,' and, 'He who curses father or mother, let him be put to death.' But you say, 'Whoever says to his father or mother, "Whatever profit you might have received from me has been dedicated to the temple"—is released from honoring his father or mother. Thus you have made the commandment of God of no effect by your tradition." Hypocrites! Well did Isaiah prophesy about you, saying: "These people draw near to me with

> their mouth and honor me with their lips, but their heart is far from Me. And in vain they worship Me, teaching as doctrines the commandments of men." The LORD knew that we could not and can not walk in the light and truth of His word while trying to keep the traditions of men.
>
> Matthew 15:1–9

> For laying aside the commandment of God, you hold the tradition of men, the washing of pitchers and cups, and many other such things you do. And He said to them, "All too well you reject the commandment of God, that you may keep your tradition. For Moses said, 'Honor your father and your mother,' and, 'He who curses father and your mother, let him be put to death.' But you say, if a man says to his father or mother, 'Whatever profit you might have received from me is Corban' (that is, dedicated to the temple); and you no longer let him do anything for his father or his mother, making the word of God of no effect through your tradition which you have handed down. And many such things you do."
>
> Mark 7:8–13

You know the great thing about God and his Word is that it never changes. Whether he is talking to the Pharisees or the church today, you can't serve the traditions of a church and the Word of God. In this paragraph, the authors go so far as to tell you that their tradition is distinct from the Sacred Scripture or Word. Then, they say, "Though closely connected to it." Well, I don't know about you, but I am not going to bet my eternal destiny on something that is closely connected to, yet different from, what the Word of God teaches!

†

Sacred Tradition and Sacred Scripture, then, are bound closely together and communicate one with the other. For both of them, flowing out from the same divine well-spring, come together in same fashion to form one thing and move towards the same goal. Each of them makes present and fruitful in the Church the mystery of Christ, who promised to remain with his own always, to the close of the age.

page 31, paragraph 80

The first part of this sentence is simply not true. You can clearly see from the Scriptures previously quoted that there is a great disparity between the traditions of men and the Word of God. In fact, you will not find the phrase Sacred Tradition in God's Word. The only things truly sacred from God's prospective are his Son, the Word, and his church. Remember, his church is not a religious institution that sits on many waters, based out of Rome, but is a person or many people who have been born of the Spirit of God. Lastly, there must have been a fork in the divine well spring or else the traditions of the Levitical priesthood would have been sufficient for us and the Catholic Church, but God sent his Son, who came in the fullness of the volume of the book, so that we might have life, liberty, and abide therein. You see, the traditions of the Catholic Church cannot stand in the light of God's Word; you must either embrace the traditions of men or throw yourself whole-heartedly after the Word of God or Jesus.

†

Sacred Scripture is the speech of God as it is put down in the writing under the breath of the Holy Spirit. And Holy Tradition transmits in its entirety the word of God which has been entrusted to the apostles by Christ the LORD *and the Holy Spirit.*

page 31, paragraph 81

I love this quote. They have a great way of saying what the Sacred Scripture is: the speech of God. The next sentence is where you find trouble; here, they change the word from *Sacred* to *Holy,* both of which cannot be found in God's Word with regard to tradition. They also go on to suggest that this supposed holy Tradition is necessary to transmit in its entirety the Word of God. Well, this sounds like a completely logical statement, except it has no support from the Bible. The Bible says of itself, in 2 Timothy 3:16–17, "All Scripture is given by inspiration of God, and is profitable for doctrine, for reproof, for correction, for instruction in righteousness, that the man of God may be complete thoroughly equipped for every good work." Notice, there is no mention of any tradition necessary for our instruction in righteousness. Also, here we see it is again, it is through the Scripture or the Word of God that we may be complete.

†

As a result the Church, to whom the transmission and interpretation of Revelation is entrusted, "does not derive her certainty about all revealed truths from the Holy Scriptures alone. Both Scripture and Tradition must be accepted and honored with equal sentiments of devotion and reverence."

page 31, paragraph 82

Once again, we get into truth and what is our basis for truth. According to God's Word, his Word is truth, and he places it above his name. "For you have magnified your word above all your name" (Psalm 138:2). He does not say he places his word and the church's tradition above his name. Proverbs 30:5–6 says, "Every word of God is pure; He is a shield to those who put their trust in Him. Do not add to His words, lest He reprove you, and you be found a liar."

When God says do not add to his Word, this means literally, traditionally or in any other form! Remember, the only standard by which we will be judged is the Word of God.! Don't be deceived into believing that tradition or anything else will be of some benefit to you when you die and are standing before the judgment seat of God! Second Thessalonians 1:8 says, "In flaming fire taking vengeance on those who do not know God, and on those who do not obey the gospel of our Lord Jesus Christ." Please take notice, there is no mention of what we do with the supposed sacred tradition, nor will you find tradition as a standard by which God uses to judge righteousness. The last part of this sentence is extremely troubling. It says, "Both Scripture and Tradition must be accepted and honored with equal sentiments of devotion and reverence." You never find Scripture and Tradition on equal footing in the Bible, and I believe I have made this point clear. Secondly, this statement is very similar to what the Pharisees did when Jesus was here. They were so caught up in their religious traditions that they missed the very one whom their Scriptures foretold would be in their midst. But, if they had read and studied the Word of God, they surely would have recognized the one whom they persecuted and crucified. You see, it is no different today than it was back then. God is calling us to worship him in spirit and truth, and his truth is found solely in his Word. Truth and tradition should never be placed on equal footing because you will end up being a double-minded person, and the Bible says that person is unstable in all their ways. James 1:8 says, "A double-minded man is unstable in all his ways." When the Bible speaks of being double-minded, it is generally talking about the flesh warring with the spirit, and the traditions of men are a type of the flesh, which makes war with the Word of God, a type of the spirit.

†

The task of giving an authentic interpretation of the word of God, whether in it's written form or in the form of tradition, has been entrusted to the living teaching office of the Church alone. It's authority in this matter is exercised in the name of Jesus Christ This means that the task of interpretation has been entrusted to the bishops in communion with the successor of Peter, the Bishop of Rome.

page 32, paragraph 85

The first part of this sentence I agree with, except one has to ask who is the church? I have previously pointed out the church is a group of born again believers in Christ, and the teaching office is the Word of God and the Holy Spirit. As for the last portion of the paragraph, I don't find any succession of interpretation being entrusted to any one group or person, particularly as it pertains to Peter. What is found in the Bible are men and women who spoke or wrote as they were instructed by the Holy Spirit, which is consistent with what the Bible teaches. In so far as interpreting the Word of God, God says he will instruct the believer in all truth according to his word. John 16:13–15 says, "However, when He, the Spirit of truth, has come, He will guide you into all truth; for whatever He hears He will speak; and He will tell you things to come, He will glorify Me, for He will take of what is Mine and declare it to you. All things that the Father has are Mine. Therefore I said that He will take of Mine and declare it to you."

> But God has revealed them to us through His Spirit. For the Spirit searches all things, yes the deep things of God. For what man knows things of

> a man except the spirit of the man which is in him? Even so no one knows the things of God except the spirit of God. Now we have received, not the spirit of the world, but the Spirit who is from God, that we might know the things that have been freely given to us by God. These things we also speak, not in words which man's wisdom teaches but which the Holy Spirit teaches, comparing spiritual things with spiritual. But the natural man does not receive the things of the Spirit of God, for they are foolishness to him; nor can he know them, because they are spiritually discerned. But he who is spiritual judges all things, yet he himself is rightly judged by no one. For "Who has known the mind of the LORD that he may instruct him?" But we have the mind of Christ.
>
> 1 Corinthians 2:10–16

John 14:26 says, "But the Helper, the Holy Spirit, whom the Father will send in my name, He will teach you all things, and bring to your remembrance all things that I said to you."

> But as for you, continue in the things which you have learned and been assured of, knowing from whom you have learned them, and that from childhood you have know the Holy Scriptures, which are able to make you wise for salvation through faith which is in Christ Jesus. All Scripture is given by inspiration of God, and is profitable for doctrine, for reproof, for correction, for instruction in righteousness, that the man of God may be complete, thoroughly equipped for every good work. I do believe the best way to interpret what the Bible says is by checking what the verse says in light of the entirety of scripture.
>
> 2 Timothy 3 14–17

†

The whole body of the faithful ... cannot err in matters of belief.

page 33, paragraph 92

This statement simply is not true. Any one faithful or unfaithful *can* err when we fall into sin or do things which are inconsistent with the Word of God.

†

It is clear therefore that, in the supremely wise arrangement of God, Sacred Tradition, Sacred Scripture, and the magisterium of the Church are so connected and associated that one of them cannot stand without the others. Working together, each in its own way, under the action of the Holy Spirit, they all contribute effectively to the salvation of souls.

page 34, paragraph 95

John 1:1–2 says, "In the beginning was the Word, and the Word was with God, and the Word was God. He was in the beginning with God." Please notice that in the beginning was the Word and the Word stood just fine without tradition or the magisterium. One thing is for sure: heaven and earth will pass away, but the Word of God will stand and stand alone. God in his sovereignty has chosen to use us, the believers in Christ or the church, but we have nothing to do with whether God's Word stands or falls. God said his Word will stand, and therefore it will stand. His Word is not dependant on tradition or the church. God, through his grace, has given us his Word so that we might be made complete and thoroughly equipped for every good work. Isaiah 40:8 says, "Surely the people are grass. The grass withers, the flower fades, but the word of our God stands forever." Matthew 24:35 says, "Heaven and earth will pass away, but My words will by no means pass away."

†

The Church, in her doctrine, life, and worship, perpetuates and transmits to every generation all that she herself is, all that she believes.

page 35, paragraph 98

The Bible is what God has left for the church to perpetuate and transmit to every generation and to the ends of the earth.

†

The task of interpreting the word of God authentically has been entrusted solely to the magisterium of the Church, that is, to the Pope and to the bishops in communion with him.

page 35, paragraph 100

Wow, then one must also conclude that holy men of God like Martin Luther, Billy Graham, Charles Stanley, and all others have been in error because they are not under the Pope. One would be hard-pressed to argue with the fact that these men have impacted the world in a profound way for the kingdom of God. They have done so by interpreting the Word of God and then preaching and teaching it. This statement is contrary to the Word of God, which says the Holy

Spirit will be our teacher who will guide us in all truth. No person should ever forfeit their God-given right to reason and discernment. God forbid, most people would never think of doing this in their daily lives (i.e., work, school and formulating their faith). Elijah was a man who was greatly troubled by the religious practices during his time. The false prophets were leading the people into idol worship, and this grieves the heart of God and, ultimately, it will bring judgment upon the leaders and the people. 1 Kings 18:21 says, "And Elijah came to all the people, and said, 'How long will you falter between two opinions? If the LORD is God, follow Him; but if Baal, then follow him.' But the people answered him not a word." Another example is found in the book of Joshua. Joshua 24:14–15, "Now therefore, fear the LORD, serve Him in sincerity and in truth, and put away the gods which your fathers served on the other side of the River and in Egypt. Serve the LORD! And if it seems evil to you to serve the LORD, choose for yourselves this day whom you will serve, whether the gods which your fathers served that were on the other side of the River, the gods of the Amorites, in whose land you dwell. But as for me and my house, we will serve the LORD." Joshua 24:24 says, "And the people said to Joshua, 'The LORD our God we will serve, and His voice we will obey.'" The LORD is seeking out those who will listen to his voice. You will not know the Shepherd's voice if you have not rightly divided his Word and you can not rightly divide his Word if you are allowing someone else to interpret the Word for you. Ezekiel 20:7 says, "Then I said to them, 'Each of you, throw away the abominations which are before his eyes, and do not defile yourselves with the idols of Egypt. I am the LORD your God.'" Ezekiel 20:18–19 says, "But I said to their children in the wilderness, 'Do not walk in the statues of your fathers, nor observe their judgments, nor defile yourselves with their idols. I am the LORD your God: Walk in My statutes, keep my judgments, and do them …'"

✝

For this reason, the Church has always venerated the Scriptures as she venerates the LORD*'s body. She never ceases to present to the faithful the bread of life, taken from the one table of God's word and Christ's body.*

page 36, paragraph 103

I'm not sure why they feel it is necessary to venerate any thing other than the LORD himself. The LORD is spirit, and those who worship him do so in spirit and truth (John 4:23). To venerate the LORD's body would mean that he was physically still here with us, and we know that this is not the case. He is seated at the right hand of the Father in heaven (Hebrews 10:12). So, to say that the church is calling the LORD's body out of heaven simply makes no sense. Especially when you consider the fact that Christ promised to leave his holy spirit with the believer and we have become new creatures in Christ Jesus. Second Corinthians 5:17 says, "Therefore, if anyone is in Christ, he is a new creation; old things have passed away; behold, all things have become new."

†

The Old Testament is an indispensable part of Scared Scripture. Its books are divinely inspired and retain a permanent value, for the Old Covenant has never been revoked.

page 40, paragraph 121

The first part of the sentence about the Old Testament is right on. The second part of the paragraph is false. Hebrews 8:7–13 and 9:1–11 clearly points out that Christ has established a new covenant.

> For if that first covenant had been faultless, then no place would have been sought for a second. Because finding fault with them, he says: "Behold, the days are coming, says the Lord, when I will make a new covenant with the house of Israel and with the house of Judah—not according to the covenant that I make with their fathers in the day when I took them by the hand to lead them out of Egypt; because they did not continue in my covenant, and I disregarded them," says the Lord. "For this is the covenant that I will make with the house of Israel after those days," says the Lord: "I will put my laws in their mind and write them on their hearts; and I will be their God, and they shall be my people. None of them shall teach his neighbor, and none his brother, saying, 'Know the Lord,' for all shall know Me, from the least of them to the greatest of them. For I will be merciful to their unrighteousness, and their sins and their lawless deeds I will remember no more," in that He says, "A new covenant," He has made the first obsolete. Now what is becoming obsolete and growing old is ready to vanish away.
>
> Hebrews 8:7–13

Then indeed, even the first covenant had ordinances of divine service and the earthly sanctuary. For a tabernacle was prepared: the first part, in which was the lamp-stand, the table, and the show bread, which is called the sanctuary; and behind the second veil, the part of the tabernacle which is called the Holiest of All, which had the golden altar of incense and the ark of the covenant overlaid on all sides with gold, in which were the golden pot that had the manna, Aaron's rod that budded, and the tablets of the covenant; and above it were the cherubim of glory overshadowing the mercy seat. Of these things we cannot now speak in detail. Now when these things had been thus prepared, the priests always went into the first part of the tabernacle, performing the services. But into the second part the high priest went alone once a year, not without blood, which he offered for himself and for the people's sins omitted in ignorance; the Holy Spirit indicating this, that the way into the Holiest of All was not yet made manifest while the first tabernacle was still standing. It was symbolic for the present time in which both gifts and sacrifices are offered cannot make him who performed the service perfect in regard to the conscience concerned only with foods and drinks, various washings, and fleshly ordinances imposed until the time of reformation. But Christ came as High Priest of the good things to come, with the greater and more perfect tabernacle not made with hands, that is, not of this creation.

Hebrews 9:1–11

Here again, you have to decide: is the Catholic Church's teaching correct or is the Word of God? Notice that the LORD says all of these things or fleshly ordinances were in place until the time of reformation. We are made complete in Christ, thus we are no longer under the law or Old Covenant. If we could have kept all these ordinances and laws, then we would have no need of Christ's sacrifice on the cross. Thank God he made provision for all who will come to him and acknowledge that we all have sinned and broken his law, which is found in the Old Covenant.

✝

The Church has always venerated the divine Scriptures as she venerated the body of the LORD *(dv21): both nourish and govern the whole Christian life. "Your word is a lamp to my feet and a light to my path" (Ps 119:105 cf Isa 50:4).*

page 44, paragraph 141

One thing is for certain, God places his Word above his name (Psalm 138:2). But, you do not see any evidence of the church venerating or worshiping the LORD's body. The believers who were here with him when he was on earth worshiped him because he was the LORD incarnate. They did not continue to worship his body after he had been crucified because, although they did not fully understand it at the time, they did come to realize that he went back to being the Spirit from which he had always been. They also came to realize that Christ became a man so that his body and blood would be the means by which he would redeem mankind. So, they were not worshiping the LORD's body, but the LORD himself while he was alive on the earth. But, after his physical death, they did not continue to worship or venerate the LORD's body because on the third day his body was resurrected. John 4:23–24 says, "But the hour is coming, and now is, when the true worshipers will worship the Father in spirit and truth; for the Father is seeking such to worship him. God is Spirit, and those who worship Him must worship in spirit and truth." So, you can clearly see by the LORD's own words that he was and still is pointing the believers in him to look to the Spirit, not the physical body. John 6:63 says, "It is the Spirit who gives life; the flesh profits nothing. The words that I speak to you are spirit and they are life."

†

To obey (from the Latin ob-audile, to "hear or listen to") in faith is to submit freely to the word that has been heard, because its truth is guaranteed by God, who is truth itself. Abraham is the model of such obedience offered us by Sacred Scripture. The Virgin Mary is its most perfect embodiment.

page 45, paragraph 144

The first part of this paragraph is true. We should submit freely to the Word because its truth is guaranteed by God. Although Abraham is a model of obedience, he still was not without sin. He did not listen to the LORD when he had promised him children. Genesis 13:16 says, "And I will make your descendants as the dust of the earth; so that if a man could number the dust of the earth, then your descendants also could be numbered." So far as Mary being the most perfect embodiment of obedience, I would suppose she is at the top of the list, along with many others who have gone before her and who are living today. But what we can't do is forget that Mary, Abraham, David, Job, Joseph, and people like Moses were not without sin. Matthew 1:21 says, "And she will bring forth a Son, and you shall call his name Jesus, for he will save his people from their sins." When considering Mary, I don't think anyone doubts that she was a great woman of faith. In fact, Luke 1:28 says, "And having come in, the angel said to her, "rejoice, highly favored one, the Lord is with you; blessed are you among women." So, the thing we must remember is that Mary was a human being just like you and I, and she was not without sin, or else she would not have been chosen by the Lord to bring Jesus into the world. There would have been no need of a savior if there was already a sinless human on earth. To be human is to be born with sin. This is why we need to be born again of the Spirit, so we have the power of God within us, who enables us to overcome sin. For this reason, I believe Christ would have to be the most perfect embodiment of obedience. He was and is the only person who was and is without sin!

†

It is through the Church that we receive faith and new life in Christ by Baptism.

page 52, paragraph 168

This is a false statement. John 6:44 says, "No one comes to Me unless the Father who sent me draws Him: and I will raise him up at the last day." Romans 10:17 says, "So then faith comes by hearing, and hearing by the word of God."

> Jesus answered and said to him, "Most assuredly, I say to you, unless one is born again, he cannot see the kingdom of God." Nicodemus said to him, "How can a man be born when he is old? Can he enter a second time into his mother's womb and be born?" Jesus answered, "Most assuredly, I say to you unless one is born of water and the Spirit, he cannot enter the kingdom of God. That which is born of the flesh is flesh, and that which is born of the Spirit is spirit. Do not marvel that I said to you, 'You must be born again.' The wind blows where it wishes, and you hear the sound of it, but cannot tell where it comes from and where it goes. So is everyone who is born of the Spirit."
>
> John 3:3–8

John 3:15–16 says, "That whoever believes in Him should not perish but have eternal life. For God so loved the world that He gave His only begotten Son, that whoever believes in Him should not perish but have everlasting life." In John 3:5, where Christ says, "unless one is born of water and the Spirit," Christ is not referring to being baptized; he is talking about being born once physically and then being born again of his Spirit or asking Christ to forgive you of your sins. So, new life in Christ has nothing to do with baptism, except that baptism would be symbolic of a person whose sins have been forgiven, and they now have risen to a new life in Christ. Don't misunderstand; no one has ever entered, nor will enter, the kingdom of God by way of a sprinkling or a pouring on of water.

†

Salvation comes from God alone; but because we receive the life of faith through the Church, she is our mother: "we believe the Church as the mother of our new birth, and not in the Church as if she were the author of our salvation." "Because she is our mother, she is also our teacher in the faith."

page 52, paragraph 169

The first part of this paragraph is where the whole paragraph should begin and end. After the first semicolon, the paragraph goes downhill. We receive Christ and have a life of faith because the Spirit draws us to himself. Romans 10:17 says, "No one comes to Me unless the Father who sent me draws him; and I will raise him up at the last day." Once again, they refer to the church as our mother, and this simply cannot be found in the Bible. Then, they go on to say, "We believe the Church as the mother of our new birth." Well, since the church is not a mother at all, but a bride, this sentence could read, "We believe the Spirit or Christ as the author and finisher our faith."

> Therefore we also, since we are surrounded by so great a cloud of witnesses, let us lay aside every weight, and the sin which so easily ensnares us, and let us run with endurance the race that is set before us, looking unto Jesus, the author and finisher of our faith, who for the joy that was set before Him endured the cross, despising the shame, and has sat down at the right hand of the throne of God.
>
> Hebrews 12:1–2

Lastly, they say, "Because she is our mother, she is also our teacher in the faith." Here again, because you simply cannot find the church being referred to as our mother, this sentence makes no sense. This sentence could correctly read, "Because Christ is our savior, he promised to leave us his Holy Spirit to guide us into all truth." John 16:13 says, "However, when He, the Spirit of truth, has come, He will guide you into all truth; for He will not speak on His own authority, but whatever He hears He will speak; and He will tell you things to come." It would appear on the basis of this paragraph that there seems to be some confusion in so far as who or what the church is within the Catholic Church. However, what is clear from God's Word is that the church is the believers in Christ, not a mother. The believers are referred to as the bride of Christ, and as the bride of Christ, God promised to leave with them his Holy Spirit and his Word, which will guide them into all truth.

†

As a mother who teaches her children to speak and so to understand and communicate, the church our mother teaches us the language of faith in order to introduce us to the understanding and life of faith.

page 53, paragraph171

This sentence could correctly read, "The Word of God inspired by the Holy Spirit teaches us the language of faith in order to introduce us to the understanding and the life of faith."

†

Believing is an ecclesial act. The Church's faith precedes, engenders, supports, and nourishes our faith. The Church is the mother of all believers." "No one can have God as father who does not have the Church as mother" (St. Cyprian, De unit.6:p14, 519).

page 55, paragraph 181

The first part of the sentence that says, "Believing is an ecclesial act," is not true. Believing is a spiritual act by which the Spirit draws whoever he has chosen unto himself. The church or group of believers may be instruments in God's hands that assist in leading someone to faith or believing in Christ. But, believing or coming to faith in Christ is a spiritual act of God, not an ecclesial act. The last part of the sentence is a statement made in ignorance. Here again, when correctly interpreting the meaning of the church, which is the bride of Christ or believers in Christ, this sentence makes no sense. Read it this way, "No one can have God as Father who does not have the bride of Christ as mother." But, let's assume this statement is correct the way it is quoted in the catechism. If no one can have God as Father who does not have the Church as mother, then how did all the Old Testament saints find there way to Father God. There was no church in the sense the authors are referring to it. How about the robber next to Jesus on the cross? He clearly did not have the Church as mother, yet Christ said today you will be with me in paradise (Luke 23:43). So, when taking an honest look at this statement, one can clearly see it is false. On page 57 in the credo toward the end, they say, "We acknowledge one baptism for the forgiveness of sins." Once again they reference baptism for the forgiveness of sins, and, as I have stated earlier, water from any church, Catholic or not, will not remove sin.

I found it rather interesting that the Catholic Church refers to itself as, "The Mother of our new birth" (paragraph 169), "The Church our Mother teaches us the language of faith in order to introduce us to the understanding and the life of faith" (paragraph 171), and, "No one can have God as Father who does not have the Church as mother" (paragraph 181). As I have pointed out earlier, the Bible never refers to the church or believers in Christ as a mother, but in Rev. 17, the Lord does describe a religious organization, which he refers to as, "The mother of harlots and of the abominations of the earth" (Rev. 17:5). He even goes so far as to tell the reader where this religious organization is based out of: "Here is the mind which has wisdom: the seven heads are seven mountains on which the woman sits" (Rev. 17:9). What has always been referred to as the city that sits on seven hills or mountains? Rome. Revelation 18:7 says, "In the measure that she glorified herself and lived luxuriously, in the same measure give her torment and sorrow; for she says in her heart I sit as queen, and am no widow and will not see sorrow." Well, by the catechism's own words in paragraph 181, the Catholic Church would be referring to itself as queen.

†

To say the credo with faith is to enter into communion with God, Father, Son, and Holy Spirit, and also with the whole Church which transmits the faith to us and in whose midst we believe: this creed is the spiritual seal, our heart's meditation and an ever-present guardian; it is, unquestionably, the treasure of our soul.

page 60, paragraph 197

The credo in and of itself is all good and true, except the part about baptism for the forgiveness of sins. Remember, baptism is an outward manifestation of an inward change. The issue is how one enters into communion with God outside a contrite and broken spirit. Psalm 51:17 says, "The sacrifices of God are a broken spirit, a broken and a contrite heart—these, O God, you will not despise." God is not interested in a bunch of vain, repetitious sayings if our hearts are not right with him. Psalm 66:18 says, "If I regard iniquity in my heart, the LORD will not hear." So, true communion with God begins with realizing I'm a sinner in desperate need of God's mercy and grace. I need a fresh outpouring of his holy spirit in my life on a daily basis. As for the credo being the spiritual seal, I find no evidence of any credo being a seal in the believer's life. I do find the believer being sealed by the Holy Spirit. Ephesians 4:30 says, "And do not grieve the Holy Spirit of God, by whom you were sealed for the day of redemption." Second Corinthians 1:22 says, "Who also has sealed us and given us the Spirit in our hearts as a deposit." The Spirit is the spiritual seal, our heart's meditation and an ever-present guardian; it is, unquestionably, the treasure of our soul." What would you rather be trusting in: a credo or a true and living God, who has left his Spirit to reside in you, if you want him to?

†

From the beginning, the revealed truth of the Holy Trinity has been at the very root of the Church's living faith, principally by means of Baptism.

page 74, paragraph 249

The revealed truth of the Holy Trinity is done by the work of the Holy Spirit in an individual's life. You see, the Bible says that the natural man cannot receive spiritual things unless the Spirit reveals it to them. This is accomplished by the Holy Spirit within the individual. The Holy Trinity will never be fully understood until we are with him in heaven. However, baptism apart from having been born again of the Spirit of God certainly does not help one in their understanding of the Holy Trinity.

> But God has revealed them to us through His Spirit. For the spirit searches all things, yes the deep things of God. For what man knows the things of a man except the spirit of the man which is in him? Even so no one knows things of God except the Spirit of God. Now we have received, not the spirit of the world, but the Spirit who is from God that we might know the things that have been freely given to us by God. These things we also speak, not in words which man's wisdom teaches, but which the Holy Spirit teaches, comparing spiritual things with spiritual. But, the natural man does not receive the things of the Spirit of God, for they are foolishness to him; nor can he know them, because they are spiritually discerned.
>
> 1 Corinthians 2:10–14

So, a person must come to faith in Christ before he has the ability to understand spiritual things, and as I pointed out earlier, no sprinkling on of water on a baby or an adult is going to help them understand the things of God.

†

By the grace of Baptism in the name of the Father and the Son and the Holy Spirit, "we are called to share in the life of the blessed trinity, here on earth in the obscurity of faith, and after death in eternal light."

page 79, paragraph 265

Here again, we must remember what Christ said in John 3:3, "Jesus answered and said to him, 'Most assuredly, I say to you, unless one is born again, he cannot enter the kingdom of God.'" You can sprinkle water in the name of the Father and the Son and the Holy Spirit all you want, but neither the water nor the names in which you sprinkle will convert that person's soul. The Word of God is quite clear with regard to this matter. People time and time again believed in Christ for their forgiveness of sin and then were baptized. Again, the order is important because you would not want someone to believe simply because they were baptized that their sins have been forgiven.

> "To Him all the prophets witness that, through His name, whoever believes in Him will receive remission of sins." While Peter was still speaking these words, the Holy Spirit fell upon all those who heard the word. And those of the circumcision that were from who believed were astonished, as many as came with Peter, because the gift of the

> Holy Spirit had been poured out on the Gentiles also. For they heard them speak with tongues and magnify God. Then Peter answered, "Can anyone forbid water, that these should not be baptized (who have received the Holy Spirit) just as we have?" and he commanded them to be baptized in the name of the LORD. Then they asked him to stay a few days.
>
> Acts 10:43–47

> Then he said, "The God of our fathers has chosen you that you should know His will, and see the just one, and hear the voice of His mouth." For you will be His witness to all men of what you have seen and heard. And now why are you waiting? Arise and be baptized, and wash away your sins, calling on the name of the LORD."
>
> Acts 22:14–16

Here Saul had just had an encounter with the Holy Spirit, and then he is instructed to be baptized. Acts 2:38 says, "Then Peter said to them, repent, and let every one of you be baptized in the name of Jesus Christ for the remission of sins; and you shall receive the gift of the Holy Spirit." Acts 2:41 says, "Then those who gladly received his word were baptized; and that day about three thousand souls were added to them." In both of these cases, the people had just received the LORD or were repenting of their sins and then were baptized.

> To Him all the prophets witness that, through His name, whoever believes in Him will receive remission of sins. While Peter was still speaking these words, the Holy Spirit fell upon all those who heard the word and those of the circumcision who believed were astonished, as many as lame with Peter, because the gift of the Holy Spirit had been

> poured out on the gentiles also. For they heard them speak with tongues and magnify God. Then Peter answered, "Can anyone forbid water, that these should not be baptized who have received the Holy Spirit just as we have?" And he commanded them to be baptized in the name of the LORD. Then they asked him to stay a few days.
>
> Acts 10: 43–48

Verse 43 clearly demonstrates how a person is first saved—"whoever believes in Him"—and then shows how the Holy Spirit still falls on those who receive his word in verses 44–45, and finally the order in which a person is to be baptized in verses 47–48. In verse 47, Peter sets the order when he says, "who have received the Holy Spirit." If Peter knew the Gentiles had not received the Holy Spirit, he would not have commanded them to be baptized.

Then, in Acts 15:1–11 it says there was a debate over keeping the law, and it says,

> And certain men came down from Judea and taught the brethren, "Unless you are circumcised according to the custom of Moses, you cannot be saved. "Therefore, when Paul and Barnabas had no small dissension and dispute with them, they determined that Paul and Barnabas and certain others of them should go up to Jerusalem, to the apostles and elders, about this question. So, being sent on their way by the church, they passed through Phoenicia and Samaria, describing the conversion of the Gentiles; and they caused great joy to all the brethren. And when they had come to Jerusalem, they were received by the church and the apostles and the elders; and they reported all things that God had

> done with them, but some of the sect of the Pharisees who believed rose up saying, "It is necessary to circumcise them, and to command them to keep the law of Moses."
>
> Acts 15:1–5

Or, in this case, "It is necessary to baptize them and to command them to keep the traditions of the Catholic Church."

> So, the apostles and elders came together to consider this matter. And when there had been much dispute, Peter rose up and said them: "Men and brethren, you know that a good while ago God choose among us, that by my mouth the Gentiles should hear the word of the gospel and believe. So, God, who knows the heart, acknowledged them, by giving them the Holy Spirit just as he did to us, and made no distinction between us and them, purifying their hearts by faith. Now therefore, why do you test God by putting a yoke on the neck of the disciples which neither our fathers nor we were able to bear?"
>
> Acts 15:6–10

In other words, why do you add anything else to what justifies a man except faith? "But, we believe that through the grace of the LORD Jesus Christ we shall be saved in the same manner as they" (Acts 15:11). So, it is through the grace of our LORD Jesus Christ and faith in him alone that we shall be saved! Later, in Acts 15, the apostles, elders, and brethren write a letter that addresses the issue of adding to faith in Christ for salvation. Acts 15:24 says, "Since we have heard that some who went out from us have troubled you with words, unsettling your souls, sayings, 'You must be circumcised and keep the law'—to whom we gave no such commandment—." I have been told that one reason for infant baptism being considered as based on the Scripture is that it says households were baptized, and that is true. But, when you look at the Scripture contextually and not just based on a single verse, you find,

> So they said, "Believe on the LORD Jesus Christ, and you will be saved, you and your household." Then they spoke the word of the LORD to him and to all who were in his house. And he took them the same hour of the night and washed their stripes. And immediately he and all his family were baptized. Now when he had brought them into his house, he set food before them; and rejoiced, having believed in God with all his household.
>
> Acts 16:31–34

What's interesting to me is that the Word says, "having believed in God with all his household.

Well, one thing we do know is that an infant does not have the ability to believe unto salvation, so the argument that there were infants in the house does not make sense.

> There is also an antitype which now saves us, namely baptism not the removal of filth of the flesh, but the answer of a good conscience toward God, through the resurrection of Jesus Christ, who has gone into heaven and is at the right hand of God, angels and authorities and powers having been made subject to Him.
>
> 1 Peter 3: 21–22

Here, Peter is referring to being born of the Spirit, and the evidence is found in Romans 10:10, which says, "For with the heart one believes to righteousness, and with the mouth confession is made to salvation." And again Paul writes,

> Or do you not know that as many of us as were baptized into Christ Jesus were baptized into his death? Therefore we were buried with Him through baptism into death, that just as Christ was raised from the dead by the glory of the Father, even so we also should walk in newness of life. For if we have been united together in the likeness of His death, certainly we also shall be in the likeness of His resurrection, knowing this, that our old man was crucified with Him, that the body of sin might be done away with, that we should no longer be slaves of sin. For he who has died has been freed from sin.
>
> Romans 6: 3–7

In these verses, Paul illustrates how baptism is a symbolic act of obedience which demonstrates the act of one dying to the old flesh nature and being raised in our new spirit nature. The newness of life referred to in verse 4, is the spirit of God which is implanted in the believer.

†

God himself created the visible world in all its richness, diversity, and order. Scripture presents the work of the creator symbolically as a succession of six days of divine "work," concluded by the "rest" of the seventh day.

page 98, paragraph 337

The first sentence starts out great, but the second sentence quickly goes down hill. There simply is no evidence to say that the account of creation is a symbolic representation of what took place. In fact, to say that the creation account is symbolic really discredits the truth and accuracy of the whole Bible. Here is why. If you say that creation is symbolic, then what's to say that the flood of Noah was symbolic or Moses parting the Red Sea was symbolic, and you could just go straight through the Bible this way.

†

In no way is God in man's image. He is neither man nor woman. God is pure spirit in which there is no place for the difference between the sexes.

page 105, paragraph 370

This is a true statement with regard to God being pure spirit, and since it is a truth, one must ask how then does the Eucharist agree or disagree with this statement? Is God always pure spirit? Now that he is seated at the right hand of the Father, is he sometimes spirit, flesh, and blood, which the Catholic Church professes to have the ability to call God out of heaven back into a cup and a wafer? He is seated at the right hand of the Father until a time when he has predetermined, to return for his church and judge the world. In the meantime, he has promised to leave a portion of his Spirit with every person who believes by faith; he is the Son of God. His Spirit is sufficient for all things pertaining to salvation. Therefore, we would have no need of a little physical Jesus supposedly found in the Eucharist.

†

Hence the Church confesses that Mary is truly "mother of God" (Theo-tokos).

page 139, paragraph 495

You have got to be extremely careful here. I'm afraid this statement could land you in a lot of hot water with God. The Scripture is very clear that there were not four: mother of God, God, Jesus, and the Word. John 1:1–2 says, "In the beginning was the Word, and the Word was with God, and the Word was God. He was in the beginning with God." Notice, the Bible does not say he and she were in the beginning with God. This sentence might truthfully read, "Hence the church confesses that Mary is truly Jesus's earthly mother."

✝

The deepening of faith in the virginal motherhood led the Church to confess Mary's real and perpetual virginity even in the act of giving birth to the Son of God made man. In fact, Christ's birth "did not diminish his mother's virginal integrity but sanctified it."

page 140, paragraph 499

And so the liturgy of the Church celebrates Mary as Aeiparthenos, the "ever-virgin." This all sounds very nice and pure, almost as though Mary was high and lifted up like Jesus, except it is false. Mary had other children besides Jesus, and the Bible makes this very clear. Matthew 13:55 says, "Is this not the carpenter's son? Is not His mother called Mary? And His brothers James, Joses, Simon, and Judas? Mark 6:3 says, "'Is this not the carpenter, the Son of Mary, and brother of James, Joses, Judas, and Simon? And are not His sisters here with us?' And they were offended at Him." Matthew 1:25 says, "And did not know her till she had brought forth her firstborn Son." This verse really tells the whole story. You could forget the names of Jesus' brothers or know nothing about them, but you can't misread, "know her till;" that means he knew her.

> While he was still talking to the multitudes, behold, His mother and brothers stood outside, seeking to speak with Him. Then one said to Him, "Look, your mother and your brothers are standing outside, seeking to speak with." But He answered and said to the one who told Him, "Who is My mother and who are My brothers. For whoever does the will of My Father in heaven is My brother and sister and mother."
>
> Matthew 12: 46–50

In these verses, it is apparent who Jesus' earthly mother and brothers were, but Jesus makes his deity very clear by saying, "Whoever does the will of My Father in heaven is My brother and sister and mother."

Now, was he saying Mary was not his earthly mother or he had no earthly half brothers? No, he was simply pointing others to the Kingdom of God. John 7:3 says, "His brothers therefore said to Him, 'Depart from here and go into Judea, that your disciples also may see the works that You are doing.'" John 7:5 says, "For even His brothers did not believe in Him." The reference for this verse is Psalm 69:8–9 which says, "I have become a stranger to My brothers, and an alien to My mother's children; because zeal for your house has eaten me up." Here again, David's psalm makes it very clear that Mary had children and Jesus had earthly half brothers. Acts 1:14 says, "These all continued with one accord in prayer and supplication, with the women and Mary the mother of Jesus, and His brothers." Besides the verses that clearly show Mary had other children, I want you just think a moment logically. How unnatural would it be for a married couple to never know each other sexually? Furthermore, it would go against God's own recipe for marriage.

> And He answered and said to them, "Have you not read that He who made them at the beginning made them male and female, and said, 'For this reason a man shall leave his father and mother and be joined to his wife, and the two shall become one flesh'? So then, they are no longer two but one flesh. Therefore what God has joined together, let no man separate."
>
> Matthew 19:4–6

Furthermore, as a man, I would have a serious issue with God if he decided to choose my wife to birth the savior of the world and said, "Oh, by the way, you can never know her sexually." What would have Joseph done with his physical desires for all those years? To say Mary is an ever-virgin goes against the Word of God, logical sense, and Jewish customs of the time.

From among the descendants of eve, God chose the Virgin Mary to be the mother of His Son. "Full of grace," Mary is "the most excellent fruit of redemption" sc 103: from the first instant of her conception, she was totally preserved from the stain of original sin and she remained pure from all personal sin throughout her life.

page 142, paragraph 508

I'm not quite sure what Bible the authors are reading from, but none of the translations I have read even remotely indicate that Mary is a sort of co-redemptress or without sin. In fact, if this paragraph is true, and it is not, then God should have stopped with the birth of Mary. God would have had no need of sending his only son out of heaven to earth if there was already a sinless person on earth. In essence, by saying Mary was without sin, you really make a mockery out of the very reason why Christ had to come to the earth. You see, "For He made Him who knew no sin to be sin for us, that we might become the righteousness of God in Him" (2 Corinthians 5:21). Even the Messianic prophecies like Isaiah 53:4–12 don't make sense if there are two sinless people to be born in the world.

> Surely He has borne our griefs and carried our sorrows; yet we esteemed Him stricken, smitten by God, and afflicted, but He was wounded for our

transgressions, He was bruised for our iniquities; the chastisement for our peace was upon Him, and by His stripes we are healed. All we like sheep have gone astray; we have turned, everyone, to his own way; and the Lord has laid on Him the iniquity of us all. He was oppressed and He was afflicted, yet he opened not His mouth; He was led as a lamb to the slaughter, and as a sheep before its shearers is silent, so He opened not His mouth. He was taken from prison and from judgment, and who will declare His generation? For He was cut off from the land of the living; for the transgressions of My people He was stricken. And they made His grave with the wicked - but with the rich at His death, because He had done no violence, nor was any deceit in His mouth. Yet it pleased the Lord to bruise Him; He has put Him to grief. When you make His soul an offering for sin, He shall see His seed, He shall prolong His days, and the pleasure of the Lord shall prosper in His hand. He shall see the travail of His soul, and satisfied. By His knowledge My righteous servant shall justify many, for He shall bear their iniquities. Therefore I will divide Him a portion with the great and He shall divide the spoil with the strong, because He poured out His soul unto death, and He was numbered with the transgressors, and He bore the sin of many and made intercession for the transgressors.

Isaiah 53: 4–12

Here again, it is very apparent that all have sinned, including Mary, and there is one who lives to make intercession for us, and his name is Jesus, not Mary.

†

Mary, the all-holy ever-virgin Mother of God, is the master work of the mission of the Son and the Spirit in the fullness of time."

page 208, paragraph 721

This sentence could correctly say, "Jesus, the all-holy Son of God is the master work of the Father reviled to us in the fullness of time."

She was, by sheer grace, conceived without sin as the most humble of creatures, the most capable of welcoming the inexpressible gift of the almighty

page 208, paragraph 722

This sentence could correctly say, "Jesus was, by sheer grace, conceived without sin as the most humble of creatures." You must remember Jesus and the Father were up in heaven, and Jesus decided to take on human flesh to redeem mankind. This should be the definition of humility. Mary, on the other hand, was never anything other than a created human being, just like you and me.

†

In Mary, the Holy Spirit fulfills the plan of the Father's loving goodness

page 208, paragraph 723

This sentence could correctly say, "In Jesus, the Holy Spirit fulfills the plan of the Father's loving goodness."

✝

Finally, through Mary, the Holy Spirit begins to bring men, the objects of God's merciful love, into communion with Christ.

page 209, paragraph 725

This sentence could correctly say, "Through Jesus Christ work on the cross, the Holy Spirit brings men the objects of God's merciful love, into communion with Christ."

At the end of this mission of the Spirit, Mary became the woman, the new Eve ("mother of the living"), the mother of the "whole Christ."

page 209, paragraph 726

You will find no biblical evidence to justify a statement like this. Mary is never referred to as, "the new eve or the mother of the living."

✝

The sole Church of Christ is that which our Savior, after his resurrection, entrusted to Peter's pastoral care, commissioning him and the other apostles to extend and rule it... This Church constitutes and organized as a society in the present world, subsists in the Catholic Church, which is governed by the successor of Peter and by the bishops in communion with him.

page 234, paragraph 816

You know, the sad part of this statement is that the authors of the catechism believe that they are the sole church of Christ. The sole church of Christ is so much bigger and more diverse than just the Catholic Church. The sole church of Christ is people sold-out for the LORD Jesus Christ and his kingdom, which cannot be found on this earth. Jesus said if you love me, obey my word, not some organized society in this present world.

> But why do you call me LORD, LORD, and do not do the things which I say? Whoever comes to Me, and hears my sayings and does them, I will show you whom he is like: he is like a man building a house, who dug deep and laid the foundation on the rock. And when the flood arose, the stream beat vehemently against that house, and could not shake it, for it was founded on the rock. But he who heard and did nothing is like a man who built a house on the earth a foundation, against which the stream beat vehemently; and immediately it fell. And the ruin of that house was great.
>
> Luke 6: 46–49

This is a great verse in many ways; first, because it shows how important God's Word is in regard to having a right relationship with him; second, because, it reveals who the rock is and they are one and the same: Jesus and his word.

†

The second Vatican council's decree on ecumenism explains: "For it is through Christ's Catholic Church alone, which is the universal help toward salvation, that the fullness of the means of salvation can be obtained."

page 234, paragraph 816

This statement could correctly read, "For it is through Christ's Holy Spirit alone, which is the universal help toward salvation." It seems the Catholic Church has confused their place and the Holy Spirit's place in the believer's life. John 6:44 says, "No one comes to Me unless the Father who sent Me draws Him; and I will raise Him up at the last day." Furthermore, the fullness of the means of salvation is obtained once by any person who asks Christ into his or her life. The Catholic Church or any other believer in Christ can be used by God to aid in bringing someone to faith in Christ, but it is still only by the Spirit by which a person is saved!

In fact, in this one and only Church of God from its very beginnings there arose certain rifts, which the Apostle strongly censures as damnable.

page 235, paragraph 817

Let's take a look at some verses that point to heresy.

> But there were also false prophets among the people, even as there will be false teachers among you, who will secretly bring in destructive heresies, even denying the Lord who brought them, and bring on themselves swift destruction. And many will follow their destructive ways, because of whom the way of truth will be blasphemed. By covetousness they will exploit you with deceptive words; for a long time their judgment has been idle, and their destruction does not slumber.
>
> 2 Peter 2:1–3

"But these, like natural brute beasts made to be caught and destroyed, speak evil of things they do not understand, and will utterly perish in their own corruption, and will receive the wages of unrighteousness, as those who count it pleasure to carouse in the daytime. They are spots and blemishes, carousing in their own deceptions while they feast with you, having eyes full of adultery and that cannot cease from sin, beguiling unstable souls. They have a heart trained in covetous practices, and are accursed children. They have forsaken the right way and gone astray, follow the way of Balaam the son of Peor, who loved the wages of unrighteousness; but he was rebuked for his iniquity: a dumb donkey speaking with a man's voice restrained the madness of the prophet. These are wells without water, clouds carried by a tempest, to whom the gloom of darkness is reserved forever. For when they speak great swelling words of emptiness, they allure through the lusts of the flesh, through licentiousness, the ones who have actually escaped from those who live in error. While they promise them liberty, they themselves are sons of corruption; for by whom person is overcome, by him also he is brought into bondage. For if, after they have escaped the pollution of the world through the knowledge of the LORD and savior Jesus Christ, they are again entangled in them and overcome, the latter end is worse for them than the beginning. For it would have been better for them not to have know the way of righteousness, than the way of righteousness, than having known it, to turn from the holy commandment delivered to them. But it has happened to them according to the true proverb: "a dog returns to his own vomit, and, a sow, having washed to her wallowing in the mire."

2 Peter 2:12–22

A reference verse for these verses is Num 22:18, which says, "Then Balaam answered and said to the servants of Balak, 'Though Balak were to give me his house full of silver and gold, I could not go beyond the word of the LORD my God, to do less or more.'" I believe these are great words to live by. If you can't find it in the Word of God, it is best to leave it alone. Certainly, you don't want to teach things that, even though they may sound good in theory, they cannot be found in the Bible. When you start down this road, you are asking for judgment.

> Go, inquire of the LORD for me, for the people and for Judah, concerning the words of this book that has been found; for great is the wrath of the LORD that is aroused against us, because our fathers have not obeyed the words of this book, to do according to all that is written concerning us.
>
> 2 Kings 22:13

> Thus says the LORD: "Behold, I will bring calamity on this place and on it's inhabitants—all the words of the book which the king of Judah has read—because they have forsaken me and burned incense to other gods, that they might provoke me to anger with all the works of their hands. Therefore, my wrath shall be aroused against this place and shall not be quenched."
>
> 2 Kings 22:16–17

Why does God bring judgment? Because we don't obey the words of his book or do the things that are not in his book as if they are. Jesus had preventive words to keep people from straying from the truth.

"Then Jesus said to those Jews who believed Him,

'If you abide in My word, you are my disciples indeed. And you shall know the truth, and the truth shall make free'" (John 8:31–32). John 8:37 says, "I know that you are Abraham's descendants, but you seek to kill me, because My word has no place in you." Then, John says:

> Why do you not understand my speech? Because you are not able to listen to My word. You are of your father the devil, and the desires of your father you want to do. He was a murderer from the beginning, and does not stand in the truth, because there is no truth in him. When he speaks a lie, he speaks from his own resources, for he is a liar and the father of it. But because I tell the truth, you do not believe Me. Which of you convicts Me of sin? And if I tell the truth, why do you not believe Me? He who is of God hears God's words; therefore you do not hear, because you are not of God. Then the Jews answered and said to Him, "Do we not say rightly that you a Samaritan and have a Demon?" Jesus answered, "I do not have a demon; but I honor My Father, and you dishonor Me. And I do not seek My own glory; there is one who seeks and judges. Most assuredly, I say to you, if anyone keeps My word he shall never see death." Then the Jews said to Him, "Now we know that you have a demon! Abraham is dead, and the prophets; and you say, 'If anyone keeps My word he shall never taste death.' Are you greater than our father Abraham, who is dead? And the prophets are dead. Whom do you make yourself out to be?" Jesus answered, "If I honor Myself, My honor is nothing. It is My Father who honors Me, of whom you say He is your God. Yet, you have not know Him, but I know Him. And I say, I do not know Him,

> I shall be a lair like you; but I do know Him and keep His word."
>
> John 8:43–55

The key to staying on track and out of heresy is found right here in John 8:55: "Yet you have not known Him, but I know Him. And if I say, 'I do not know Him,' I shall be a liar like you; but I do know Him and keep His word.'" You see, God does not care what you're previous or current traditions are. He knew Paul, and he knows you and I were going to be born into whatever faith we were born into. But, his call to you and me is to lay aside the traditions of our fathers and to follow hard and fast after the whole counsel of God! I believe what breaks God's heart is that we more than ever have God's Word in so many variations—print, radio, on the computer—and yet most people will not take the time to see if the things they're practicing are found in God's revelation of himself. You know, I heard a great illustration as it pertains to this matter, and it goes like this: If a pilot told you that in order to fly from Baltimore to California that he thinks he will start out by heading to New York and on to Alaska, then back to Florida and then maybe to Detroit, you probably would consider getting off the plane, wouldn't you? If you would not be so careless with simply flying to another state, then why in the world would you be so careless with eternal matters? You owe it to yourself and to God to check his Word to see if the things which you are being told are true, are really true. Remember, Jesus said, "I am the way the truth and the life, no one comes to the Father except through Me" (John 14:6). Jesus and his Word are synonymous with each other. Know Jesus; know his Word. The Jews were very faithful to their Jewish traditions during Jesus' time on earth and missed his visitation because they were unfamiliar with his Word. If they had simply studied all the prophesies pointing directly to him, they surely would have know he was the Messiah. Instead, they remained faithful to their traditions that could not and did not save them.

✝

The Church is one : she acknowledges one LORD, *confesses one faith, is born of one baptism, forms only one body, is given life by the one Spirit, for the sake of one hope (cf Eph* 4:3–5*), at whose fulfillment all divisions will be overcome.*

page 250, paragraph 866

Here, they quote Ephesians 4:3–5, except they change the words, which completely changes the meaning of the text. Here are the verses in there entirety: "Endeavoring to keep the unity of the Spirit in the bond of peace. There is one body and one Spirit, just as you were called in one hope of your calling; one LORD, one faith, one baptism." You see, when you add, "is born of," you can get an entirely different meaning from being baptized. I think the best reference for this paragraph is Revelation 22:18, "For I testify to everyone who hears the words of the prophecy of this book: if anyone adds to these things, God will add to him the plagues that are written in this book."

✝

Her holiness shines in the saints; in Mary she is already all holy.

page 250, paragraph 867

Reference previous paragraphs on Mary.

✝

The Church is catholic: she proclaims the fullness of the faith. She bears in herself and administers the totality of the means of salvation

page 250, paragraph 868

Pardon me, so if someone believes in Christ and is born of the Spirit of God, then they would have no hope of heaven if they were not Catholic? Salvation is the free gift of God given to whomever the Spirit wishes, and for the authors to suggest that they or a church have cornered the market on the gifts of the Spirit would be a gross error on their part. Romans 3:24–25 says, "Being justified freely by His grace through the redemption that is in Christ Jesus."

†

The Virgin Mary… is acknowledged and honored as being truly the Mother of God and of the redeemer… she is clearly the mother of the members of Christ… since she has by her charity joined in bringing about the birth of believers in the church, who are members of its head. Mary, Mother of Christ, Mother of the Church.

page 273, paragraph 963

If you say Mary is the mother of God, then the Bible you have may as well be thrown in the trash. One of God's names is, "I Am," and I Am means that he always was and will be. If you suggest that Mary was the "I Was" before the I Am, then the Bible you and I have is not worth the paper it is printed on. Exodus 3:14 says, "And God said to Moses, 'I Am who I Am.' And God said, 'Thus you shall say to the children of Israel, I Am has sent me to you.'" John 8:57–58 says, "Then the Jews said to Him, 'You are not yet fifty years old, and have you seen Abraham?' Jesus said to them, 'Most assuredly, I say to you, before Abraham was, I Am.'" So, here you have both Father God and Jesus referring to themselves as "I Am." Now all you have to do is decide who is right: Father God and Jesus or the Catholic Church? By the very meaning of "I Am," which means self-existence, you can't have the God of the Bible and the Mary of the Catholic Church!

✝

Finally the Immaculate Virgin, preserved free from all stain of original sin, when the course of her earthly life was finished, was taken up body and soul into heavenly glory, and exalted by the Lord *as Queen over all things, so that she might be the more fully conformed to her Son, the* Lord *of* Lords *and conqueror of sin and death.*

page 274, paragraph 966

In so far as Mary being sinless, I have already addressed that, but now they say she was assumed into heaven and then made "Queen over all things." Well, ask yourself this question. If there were only two sinless people to ever live on earth and one of them goes on or, as it would be, back to heaven and is made, "Queen over all things," don't you think God would have at least mentioned one of these events in the Bible? Yet, there is no mention in the Bible of Mary being without original sin or being assumed into heaven. If Mary is without sin, then Adam's sin, and every other person's sin born after him, should be brought into question. But, the good news is we don't have to wonder about this issue because God's Word clearly shows us that, "All have sinned and fallen short of the glory God" (Romans 3:23). The assumption that just because the Lord used Mary as the mother of Jesus makes her without sin is simply without merit.

✝

Therefore the Blessed Virgin is invoked in the Church under the titles of Advocate, Helper, Benefactress, and Mediatrix."

page 274, paragraph 969

The titles "Advocate" and "Helper" are titles which always refer to Jesus, never Mary, in the Bible. "Benefactress" and "Mediatrix," you simply will not find any mention of such a title given to Mary or any other person in the Bible.

✝

All who die in God's grace and friendship, but still imperfectly purified, are indeed assured of their eternal salvation; but after death they undergo purification, so as to achieve the holiness necessary to enter the joy of heaven.

page 291, paragraph 1030

Listen, we are born of the Spirit of God or we are not. If we are born of the Spirit, then we will be with him in heaven because of God's grace or unmerited favor. It has nothing to do with how holy I am on my own; but through his Holy Spirit in me, I am made holy as he is holy. God no longer sees unholy Mark, but sees holy Mark, made holy by his Son's Spirit living in me. The only purification necessary to get to heaven is having God's Spirit imparted to you!

> And be found in Him, not having my own righteousness, which is from the law, but that which is through faith in Christ, the righteousness which is

> from God by faith; that I may know Him and the power of His resurrection, and the fellowship of His sufferings, being conformed to his death.
>
> Philippians 3:9–10

†

The Church gives the Purgatory to this final purification of the elect, which is entirely different from the punishment of the damned. The Church formulated her doctrine of faith on Purgatory especially at the councils of Florence and Trent. The tradition of the Church, by reference to certain texts of Scripture, speaks of a cleansing fire.

page 291, paragraph 1031

I don't know much about the councils of Florence and Trent, but I do know something about the Word of God, and there are no Scriptures that support this idea of purgatory in the Bible. You know, about the only thing that comes to mind, in so far as fire and the believer are concerned, is that our works will be tried by fire, and anything that was not done as unto the Lord will be burned up, and only the things done as unto him will last! This Bible passage is speaking of those saved and is talking about our heavenly rewards. Although, there is another fire that the Lord will send upon the people of the earth. This fire is not to winnow or to cleanse, but to render judgment. Isaiah 66:15–16 says, "See, the Lord is coming with fire, and his chariots are like a whirlwind; He will bring down His anger with fury, and His rebuke with flames of fire. For with fire and His sword the Lord will execute judgment upon all men, and many will be those slain by the LORD." Psalm 21:9 says, "You shall make them as a fiery oven in the time of your anger; The LORD shall swallow them up in His wrath, And the fire shall devour them." The good news is this, God has not appointed us to wrath. 1 Thessalonians 5:9–10 says, "For God did not appoint us to suffer wrath but to receive salvation through our LORD Jesus Christ. He died for us, that whether we wake or sleep, we should live together with Him."

> Each one's work will become manifest; for the Day will declare it, because it will be revealed by fire; and the fire will test each one's work, of what sort it is. If anyone's work which he has built on it endures, he will receive a reward. If anyone's work is burned, he will suffer loss; but he himself will be saved, yet so as through fire.
>
> 1 Corinthians 3:13–15

†

This teaching is also based on the practice of prayer for the dead, already mentioned in Sacred Scripture: "Therefore (Judas Maccabeus) made atonement for the dead, that they might be delivered from their sin. From the beginning the Church has honored the memory of the dead and offered prayers in sufferage for them, above all the Eucharistic sacrifice, so that, thus purified, they may attain the beatific vision of God. The Church also commends alms giving, indulgences, and works of penance undertaken on behalf of the dead: let us help and commemorate them. If Job's sons were purified by their father's sacrifice, why would we doubt that our offerings bring them some consolation?

Let us not hesitate to help those who have died and to offer our prayer for them."

page 291, paragraph 1032

Once again, there is no evidence of men praying for the dead that they might be delivered from their sin. The book of Maccabeus was rejected as part of the canon of Scripture. If anything, Scripture points us to pray for the living while they still have a chance to repent of their sins. Hebrews 9:27 says, "And as it appointed for men to die once, but after this the judgment." If there was a place called purgatory, and there is not, then Heb 9:27 does not make sense. Furthermore, no Eucharistic sacrifice, almsgiving, indulgences, or works of penance convert a soul from dead to living. The only thing that will convert your soul from being dead to alive is Christ's Spirit in you!

Lastly, there is no evidence in the book of Job that says anything about Job's sons being purified by Job's sacrifice. Job 1:5 says,

> So it was, when the days of feasting had run their course, that Job would send and sanctify them, and he would rise early in the morning and offer burnt offerings according to the number of them all. For Job said, "It may be that my sons have sinned and cursed God in their hearts" thus Job did regularly.
>
> Job 1:5

First, you notice that his sons are alive, and he offered burnt offerings to God, as we might offer up prayers to God for those whom we want to see God's mercy and grace poured out on them. The bottom line is this: either you are in Christ by faith or you are not.

If you are in Christ, you will be with him in heaven, and if you are not in Christ, he will say depart form me, I never knew you. There is no limbo with God. He knows our hearts and our every thought, so it will be very apparent to him which of us are his and which of us are not.

✝

Those who die in God's grace and friendship imperfectly purified, although they are assured of their eternal salvation, undergo a purification after death, so as to achieve the holiness necessary to enter the joy of God.

page 297, paragraph 1054

The first part of this sentence does not make sense in the light of Christ. First of all, how is one purified? We are purified by Christ's finished work on the cross. Hebrews 9:11–28 says,

> But Christ as High Priest of the good things to come, with the greater and more perfect tabernacle not made with hands, that is, not of this creation. Not with the blood of goats and calves, but with His own blood He entered the most holy place once for all, having obtained eternal redemption. For if the blood of bulls and goats and the ashes of a heifer, sprinkling the unclean, sanctifies for the purifying of the flesh, how much more shall the blood of Christ, who through the eternal Spirit offered without spot to God, purge your conscience from dead works to serve the living God?

You see, in this verse God is saying Eucharistic sacrifice, almsgiving, indulgences, and the works of penance are dead works. Picking up in verse 15, we read:

> And for this reason He is the Mediator of the new covenant, by means of death, for the redemption of the transgressions under the first covenant, that those who are called may receive the promise of eternal inheritance. For where there is a testament, there must also of necessity be the death of the testator. For a testament is in force after men are dead, since it has no power at all while the testator lives. Therefore not even the first covenant was dedicated without blood. For when Moses had spoken every percept to all the people according to the law, he took the blood of calves and goats, with water, scarlet wool, and hyssop, and sprinkled both the book itself and all the people, saying, "This is the blood of the covenant which God has commanded you." Then likewise he sprinkled with blood both the tabernacle and all the vessels of the ministry. And according to the law almost all things are purged with blood. And without shedding of blood there is no remission. Therefore it was necessary that the copies of the things in the heavens should be purified with these, but the heavenly things themselves with better sacrifices than these. For Christ has not entered the holy place made with hands, which are copies of the true, but into heaven itself, now to appear in the presence of God for us; not that he should offer himself often as the high priest enters the most holy place every year with blood of another.

Could verse 25 mean that there is no need of a Eucharistic sacrifice? Because, then we would be offering him often? Picking up in verse 26,

> He then would have had to suffer often since the foundation of the world; but now, once at the end of the ages, He appeared to put away sin by the sacrifice of Himself. And as it is appointed for men to die once, but after this the judgment, so Christ was offered once to bear the sins of many.
>
> Hebrews 9:26–28

I have another question: if Christ was offered once to bear the sins of many, then why would the Catholic Church offer him daily, in the Eucharistic sacrifice, for the remission of sins? Picking up in verse 28, "To those who eagerly wait for Him He will appear a second time, apart from sin, for salvation." The question one has to ask one's self in relation to this doctrine on purgatory is this: Was Christ's finished work on the cross enough to thoroughly cleanse me of my sin, or do I need the help of man and his works to help justify me in the sight of a holy and just God who has already come to earth and died for all my sins? Isaiah 44:22 says, "I have blotted out, like a thick cloud, your transgressions, and like a cloud, your sins. Return to Me, for I have redeemed you." Isaiah 43:25 says, "I, even I, am He who blots out your transgressions for My own sake; and I will not remember your sins." Micah 7:18–19 says, "He does not retain His anger for ever, because He delights in mercy. He will again have compassion on us, and will subdue our iniquities. You will cast all our sins into the depths of the sea." Jeremiah 31:34 says, "No more shall every man teach his neighbor, and every man his brother, saying, 'Know the LORD, for they all shall know Me, from the least of them to the greatest of them, says the LORD. For I will forgive their iniquity, and their sins I will remember no more.'" Psalm 103:11–12 says, "For as the heavens are high above the earth, so great is his mercy toward those who fear Him. As far as the east is from the west, so far He removed our transgressions from us." Isaiah 38:17 says, "Indeed it was for my own peace that I had great bitterness; but you have lovingly delivered my soul from the pit of corruption, for you have cast all my sins behind your back." You see, when God looks on the believers in Christ, he no longer sees their sin but the shed blood of Christ that covered all their sins once and for all. Praise God!

†

Adhering to the teaching of the Holy Scriptures, to the apostolic traditions, and to the consensus of the fathers," we profess that, "the sacraments of the new law were all instituted by Jesus Christ our LORD."

page 315, paragraph 1114

The sacraments or Christian rites, like baptism and matrimony, are things that Jesus has said we should do. Marriage is optional if you don't have the gift of celibacy. But, to put people under a supposed new law simply does not line up with Scripture.

Galatians 3:19–29 says,

> What purpose then does the law serve? It was added because of transgressions, till the seed should come to whom the promise was made; and

> it was appointed through angels by the hand of a mediator, now a mediator does not mediate for one only, but God is one. Is the law then against the promises of God? Certainly not! For if there had been a law given which could have given life, truly righteousness would have been by the law. But the Scripture has confined all under sin that the promise by faith in Jesus Christ might be given to those who believe, but before faith came, we were kept for the faith which would afterward be revealed. Therefore, the law was our tutor to bring us to Christ, that we might be justified by faith, but after faith has come, we are no longer under a tutor. For you are all sons of God through faith in Christ Jesus.

These verses make it quite clear that after we have come to Jesus in faith, there is no law or new law we are under.

✝

The Church affirms that for believers the sacraments of the New Covenant are necessary for salvation. Sacramental grace is the grace of the Holy Spirit, given by Christ and proper to each sacrament.

page 319, paragraph 1129

Here again, the authors would be guilty of adding to the Word of God. As I stated earlier, it is by the grace of God and faith in his finished work on the cross alone which gives us access to heaven. You will absolutely not find any reference to needing any such sacraments or sacramental grace in order to gain salvation in the Bible.

He gives new meaning to the deeds and signs of the Old Covenant, above all to the Exodus and the Passover, for He Himself is the meaning of all these signs.

page 325, paragraph 1151

Sacramental signs. Since Pentecost, it is through the sacramental signs of His Church that the Holy Spirit carries on the work of sanctification. The sacraments of the Church do not abolish but purify and integrate all the richness of the signs and symbols of the cosmos and of social life. Further, they fulfill the types and figures of the Old Covenant, signify and make actively present the salvation wrought by Christ, and prefigure and anticipate the glory of heaven."

page 325, paragraph 1152

In paragraph 1151, when they refer to the old covenant, they say, "For He Himself is the meaning of all these signs," and they are correct in saying so. All of the sacrifice and rituals which they performed would finally be done away with once he had come in the flesh and performed his finished work on the cross! Paragraph 1152 starts out on a sad note, because apparently the authors are under the misconception that the Holy Spirit is in need of their sacramental signs to carry on the work of sanctification. As I stated earlier, we are sanctified solely by the Holy Spirit; we cannot add to it or take away from it any of the credit due to the Holy Spirit. In the sanctification process, we can only hope that God will allow us to be used by the Holy Spirit to lead others to him! The works of men's hands have never been able to purify men or women's souls. It is only by the Holy Spirit alone in which this is accomplished! Lastly, why would you need someone to signify and "make actively present the salvation wrought by Christ" if you have that salvation presently living inside of you? You know, the great thing about knowing you are saved, sanctified, and set apart for his glory is that you don't need any sacramental signs to help you realize that you are a child of God. Furthermore, the Catholic Church cannot "make actively present the salvation wrought by Christ." You could correctly say Christ is actively present in the believer and therefore we carry the salvation which was wrought by Christ.

✝

Holy Baptism is the basis of the whole Christian life, the gateway to life in the Spirit (vitae spiritualis ianua), and the door which gives access to the sacraments. Through Baptism we are freed from sin and reborn as sons of God; we become members of Christ, are incorporated into the Church and made sharers in her mission: "Baptism is the sacrament of regeneration through water in the word."

page 342, paragraph 1213

If this statement is true, and it is not, then where would baptism fit in the lives of Abraham, Moses, and other like men and women of faith? These people were not baptized and were saved the same way you or I are saved, and that is through faith alone in God. Through the Spirit we are freed from sin and reborn of his spirit as sons of God. In the Gospel of Luke, the thief on the cross is speaking to Jesus. Jesus forgives him and assures him of paradise without baptism. Reference Luke 23: 39–43.

†

Baptism because sin is buried in the water. Through faith in Christ our sin is buried with Him and as He rose from the dead, so to we are risen to newness of life with Him.

page 342, paragraph 1216

The Church has seen in Noah's ark a prefiguring of salvation by Baptism, for by it "a few, that is, eight persons, were saved through water"

page 343, paragraph 1219

Here again, the authors completely miss the point by which Noah and his family were saved. They were not saved by the floodwaters, but spared from them because they moved with godly fear and faith in what God said would happen. If Noah, or any of us, didn't have the same faith in God through the provision of his Son's death through the cross, we would all be subjected to physical and spiritual death in the life to come.

†

The blood and water that flowed from the pierced side of the crucified Jesus are types of Baptism and the Eucharist, the sacraments of new life.

page 345, paragraph 1225

Jesus' blood and water that flowed from his pierced side are the means by which we are able to be saved. Without his sinless blood being shed, there would be no remission of sin! This is the bottom line. Without Christ's sinless blood being shed, there would be no remission of sin (Hebrews 9:22). You can place your faith in the sacramental works of a church if you choose to, but these will never bring about your remission of sin. We don't re-crucify Christ for our sins when we are baptized or take communion; we simply proclaim what he has already done for us.

✝

The Baptized have put on Christ. Through the Holy Spirit, Baptism is a bath that purifies, justifies, and sanctifies.

page 345, paragraph 1227

Through the Holy Spirit, one is purified, justified, and sanctified. Baptism simply proclaims that we have died to sin and risen in newness of life with him.

✝

From the time of the apostles, becoming a Christian has been accomplished by a journey and initiation in several stages.

page 346, paragraph 1229

There are not several stages to becoming a Christian. The only necessary thing to become a Christian is for you to realize you're a sinner and need a savior. Jesus came sinless, and he died to take away your sins, if you will ask him into your heart. Once you have done this, you are a Christian. If you want to grow in your Christian faith, you will need to know his Word, and you have to learn to abide in his spirit, which is a daily process.

†

The essential rite of the sacrament follows: Baptism properly speaking. It signifies and actually brings about death to sin and entry into the life of the most Holy Trinity through configuration to the Paschal mystery of Christ.

page 348, paragraph 1239

The rebuttal to this false statement is found in 1 Peter 1: 22–25.

> Since you have purified your souls in obeying the truth through the Spirit in sincere love of the brethren, love one another fervently with a pure heart. Having been born again, not of corruptible seed but incorruptible, through the word of God which lives and abides forever, because "all flesh is as grass, and all the glory of man as the flower of the grass. The grass withers, and its flower falls away, but the word of the LORD endures forever."
>
> 1 Peter 1: 22–25

The only thing that brings about death to sin is having been born of the spirit of God and then obeying the truth through the power the Holy Spirit, which lives and abides in you.

†

First Holy Communion. Having become a child of God clothed with the wedding garment, the neophyte is admitted "to the marriage supper of the Lamb" and receives the food of the new life, the body and blood of Christ

page 349, paragraph 1244

By all accounts, according to the Word of God, the believer's spiritual food would be the Word of God. The Word builds up the Spirit and enables us to stand against the world and allows us to be rooted and grounded in truth. Furthermore, Christ shed his blood and sacrificed his body for our sins. So is the Catholic Church saying we also need to eat Christ's body and drink his blood, as if this would be of some spiritual benefit to us? I think not. If Christ's spirit imparted to you is not enough for the complete remission of your sins, then his recreated physical body and blood certainly would not accomplish this task. Matthew 4:4 says, "But He answered and said, 'It is written, "Man shall not live by bread alone, but by every word that proceeds from the mouth of God."'"

Hebrews 5:12–14 says,

> For though by this time you ought to be teachers, you need someone to teach you again the first principles of the oracles of God; and you have come to need milk and not solid food. For everyone who partakes only of milk is unskilled in the word of righteousness, for he is a babe. But solid food belongs to those who are of full age, that is, those who by reason of use have their senses exercised to discern both good and evil.

And again, Hebrews 6:1–5 says,

> Therefore, leaving the discussion of the elementary principles of Christ, let us go on to perfection, not laying again the foundation of repentance from dead works and of faith toward God, of the doctrine of baptisms, of laying on of hands, of resurrection of the dead, and of eternal judgment. And this we will do if God permits. For it is impossible for those who were once enlightened, and have tasted the heavenly gift, and have become partakers of the Holy Spirit, and have tasted the good word of God and the powers of the age to come.

Please notice, God says we are partakers of the Holy Spirit and have tasted the good word; these are spiritual things not physical acts. First Peter 2:1–6 says,

> Therefore, laying aside all malice, all guile, hypocrisy, envy, and all evil speaking, as newborn babes, desire the pure milk of the word, that you may grow thereby, if indeed you have tasted that the Lord is gracious. Coming to Him as to a living stone, rejected indeed by men, but chosen by God and precious, you also, as living stones, are being built up a spiritual house, a holy priesthood, to offer up spiritual sacrifices acceptable to God through Jesus Christ. Therefore it is also contained in the Scripture, "Behold, I lay in Zion a chief cornerstone, elect, precious, and he who believes on Him will by no means be put to shame."

So, by these verses you can see that the believers are in the Word of God, and if you are not in His Word, then you are spiritually starving yourself to death. Meaning, your spirit cannot grow in the truth and knowledge of God. First Peter 2:1 best describes the believer's food of the new life, where it says, "Desire the pure milk of the word, that you may grow thereby."

✝

The Church and the parents would deny a child the priceless grace of becoming a child of God were they not to confer Baptism shortly after birth.

page 350, paragraph 1250

Neither the church nor the parents can deny a child the free gift of becoming a child of God, because it is by the spirit of God that a child or an adult is able to be called a child of God. So, to suggest that a child is not a child of God prior to the age of reason is simply not true. Does a parent have the responsibility to raise a child in the knowledge of God and his Word? Absolutely! Will a parent have to give an account for the knowledge of God that was imparted to them and how they instructed their children? For sure. Will a parent be sadly mistaken if they tell their child that they are saved because they were baptized as an infant? Without a doubt. This is why one must study the Word of God to see if the things they are being taught are even found in the Word. How terrible would it be if the very thing you were taught or thought was going to save your soul and you died and found out it was not true. An example of this could be a Muslim who was raised a Muslim and loved his parents, who encouraged him to become a martyr for his faith. Just because this person was taught they would go to heaven does not mean that they will reach their desired destination. As I stated earlier, the example in Scripture is that people believed and were baptized, and there is no example of an infant being baptized shortly after birth. Is it possible that by the Catholic Church implementing this practice, which is not found in Scripture, could be the very means by which they hope to keep people and their children in and under the control of their church? Furthermore, if this principle, that a child is saved by their sprinkling on of water, is false, then one must ask the question, what other teachings are false? You see, it is my conviction that God takes things that we teach as truth very seriously, and why shouldn't he? Billions of peoples souls are at stake.

✝

Baptism is the source of that new life in Christ from which the entire Christian life springs forth.

page 351, paragraph 1254

This sentence could correctly read, "Faith in Christ is the source of that new life in Christ from which the entire Christian life springs forth."

✝

The Church finds the reason for this possibility in the universal saving will of God and the necessity of Baptism for salvation.

page 352, paragraph 1256

This statement is proven false by taking the whole counsel of God and to what Jesus said to the criminal on the cross, "And Jesus said to him, 'Assuredly, I say to you, today you will be with me in paradise'" (Luke 23:43). Jesus would not have said to a criminal, who, from what we know about him was a criminal his whole life, "You are saved based on your understanding of who I am." This is important because this man, by all appearances, was a sinner his whole life.

✝

For catechumens who die before their Baptism, their explicit desire to receive it, together with repentance for their sins, and charity, assures them the salvation that they were not able to receive through the sacrament.

page 352, paragraph 1259

So, wait a minute. Is it baptism, desire for baptism, acts of charity, or repentance that assures a person salvation? Clearly, you can see how all this becomes quite confusing when you add to what God says saves a soul. The only necessary thing for salvation is repenting and believing in Jesus Christ!

✝

Let the children come to me, do not hinder them, allow us to hope that there is a way of salvation for children who have died without Baptism. All the more urgent is the church's call not to prevent little children coming to Christ through the gift of holy Baptism.

page 353, paragraph 1261

First of all, in this quote by Jesus, "Let the children come to me, do not hinder them," Jesus was speaking to his disciples, telling them to allow the children to come up to him. This was in no way related to baptizing them. Furthermore, what kind of God would send a child to hell because they were not baptized by the Catholic Church, or any other church? You don't have to hope that there is a way for children to be saved if they have not been baptized; you can be sure that God will not forsake them. But on the other hand, if you teach a child that they are saved because they were baptized as infants, you will have to give an account to God for having misled them into believing in the works of man rather than the living God.

By Baptism all sins are forgiven, original sin and all personal sins, as well as all punishment for sin.

page 353, paragraph 1263

By faith, all sins are forgiven.

✝

Baptism not only purifies from all sins, but also makes the neophyte "a new creature," an adopted son of God, who has become a partaker of the divine nature, member of Christ and co-heir with him, and a temple of the Holy Spirit.

page 354, paragraph 1265

Here again, the correct words for baptism would be *faith in Christ.* Look, an infant cannot reason, and since it cannot reason, it cannot have faith; and without faith you are simply performing a dead work. Hebrews 11:6 says, "But without faith it is impossible to please Him, for he who comes to God must believe that He is, and that He is a rewarder of those who diligently seek Him." Romans 5:1–2 says, "Therefore, having been justified by faith we have peace with God through our LORD Jesus Christ. Through whom also we have access by faith into this grace in which we stand, and rejoice in hope of the glory of God." Galatians 5:5–7 says, "For we through the Spirit eagerly wait for the hope of righteousness by faith. For in Christ Jesus neither circumcision nor uncircumcision avails anything, but faith working through love." You can clearly see that God is not interested in a person or an infant being baptized if there is not faith in him first.

Galatians 3:1–3 says,

> O foolish Galatians! Who has bewitched you that you should not obey the truth, before whose eyes Jesus Christ was clearly portrayed among you as crucified? This only I want to learn from you: did you receive the Spirit by works of the law, or by the

> hearing of faith? Are you so foolish? Having begun in the Spirit, are you now being made perfect by the flesh?

Are you now being made perfect by baptism (a work of the flesh)?

> Have you suffered so many things in vain if indeed it was in vain? Therefore He who supplies the Spirit to you and works miracles among you, does He do it by the works of the law, or by the hearing of faith? Therefore, know that (only those who are of faith) are sons of Abraham. And the Scripture, foreseeing that God would justify the nations by faith preached the gospel to Abraham beforehand, saying, "In you all the nations shall be blessed." So then those who are of faith are blessed with believing Abraham.
>
> Galatians 3:4–9

†

Baptism makes us members of the body of Christ:

page 354, paragraph 1267
Faith makes us members of the body of Christ.

†

By Baptism they share in the priesthood of Christ, in his prophetic and royal mission."

page 355, paragraph 1268

At the end of the paragraph, the authors also say, "Baptism gives a share in the common priesthood of all believers." In both of these sentences, the correct word would be *faith* instead of *baptism.*

†

Baptism constitutes the foundation of communion among all Christians, including those who are not yet in full communion with the Catholic Church.

page 355, paragraph 1271

Insert faith for baptism in this sentence as well.

†

Baptism seals the Christian with the indelible spiritual mark of his belonging to Christ.

page 356, paragraph 1272

Insert faith for baptism again.

Second Corinthians 1:22 says, "Who also has sealed us and given us the Spirit in our hearts as a deposit." And, Eph 4:30 says, "And do not grieve the Holy Spirit of God, by whom you were sealed for the day of redemption." Would you rather be trusting in the work of a priest, who baptized you, for the redemption of your soul or trusting in the Holy Spirit, which will seal you until the day of redemption?

†

Given once for all, Baptism cannot be repeated.

page 356, paragraph 1272

Christ offered himself once for all. Hebrews 10:10–14 says,

> By that will we have been sanctified through the offering of the body of Jesus Christ once for all. And very priest stands ministering daily and offering repeatedly the same sacrifices, which can never take away sins. But this man, after He had offered one sacrifice for sins forever, sat down at the right hand of God, from that time waiting till his enemies are made his footstool. For by one offering he has perfected forever those who are being sanctified.

One thing I find noteworthy is that they say baptism cannot be repeated, and yet they repeat the Eucharistic sacrifice daily, as if there would be some spiritual benefit to the believer, and yet God has said by his sacrifice alone that our sins are forgiven for those who believe. The reference the authors are referring to comes from Heb 10:10–14, and these verses are speaking about Christ having offered himself once for all, not a baptism which cannot be repeated. Furthermore, anyone who has been baptized as an infant should be baptized after they have come to the saving knowledge of God in accordance with the work of God. Lastly, nowhere does the Word say someone cannot be baptized more than once.

†

Baptism indeed is the seal of eternal life.

page 356, paragraph 1274

The Holy Spirit indeed is the seal of eternal life.

†

Christian initiation is accomplished by three sacraments together: Baptism which is the beginning of new life; confirmation which is it's strengthening; and the Eucharist which nourishes the disciple with Christ's body and blood for his transformation in Christ.

page 356, paragraph 1275

Christian initiation is accomplished by faith in Christ alone. You are strengthened by spending time in God's Word and in prayer. So, they are also saying the believer needs the physical Jesus for their transformation in Christ. The only problem with this idea is that the Bible teaches that we are transformed by the renewing of our minds in the Word and through praying to the Holy Spirit. Titus 3:5 says, "Not by works of righteousness which we have done, but according to His mercy He saved us, through the washing of regeneration and renewing of the Holy Spirit." Colossians 3:10 says, "And have put on the new man who is renewed in knowledge according to the image of Him who created him." Ephesians 4:23–24 says, "And be renewed in the spirit of your mind, and that you put on the new man which was created according to God in righteousness and true holiness." Romans 7:6 says,

"But now we have been delivered from the law, having died to what we were held by, so that we should serve in the newness of the Spirit and not in the oldness of the letter."

Galatians 2:20 says, "I have been crucified with Christ; it is no longer I who live, but Christ lives in me; and the life which I now live in the flesh I live by Faith in the Son of God, who loved me and gave Himself for me."

If Christ lives in us and has promised to never leave us, then why would you need some physical Jesus as well? You see, it is by faith that we are born of his Spirit; it is by his Spirit that we are being transformed into his likeness, and it is by his Spirit that we will be with Him in heaven! Furthermore, John 4:23–24 does not make sense if you are worshiping Jesus in a physical way: "But the hour is coming, and now is, when the true worshipers will worship the Father in spirit and truth; for the Father is seeking such to worship Him. God is Spirit, and those who worship him must worship in spirit and truth."

†

Baptism is birth into the new life in Christ. In accordance with LORD*'s will, it is necessary for salvation, as the Church herself, which we enter by Baptism.*

page 357, paragraph 1277

The Spirit gives us birth into the new life in Christ. We have already covered what is necessary for salvation. To suggest that the Catholic Church or baptism is necessary for salvation, you make it sound like God is dependant on man in order that people might be saved. This simply is a misrepresentation of God being dependant on man or a work done by man. God has no need of man in order to save a person's soul, but rather man has a great need for the spirit of God to be poured out on him so he can be forgiven his sins! To say that the Catholic Church is necessary for salvation is to limit God, or to become equal with God. Think about this. The one who created us, the heavens, and earth would then be limited by the very thing he created. Certainly not! Isaiah 64:8 says, "But now, O LORD, you are our Father; we are the clay, and you our potter; and all we are the work of your hand."

✝

The fruit of Baptism, or Baptismal grace, is a rich reality that includes forgiveness of original sin and all personal sins, birth into the new life by which man becomes an adoptive son of the Father, a member of Christ and a temple of the Holy Spirit.

page 357, paragraph 1279

By faith in the Holy Spirit, one receives forgiveness of original sin and all these other things.

✝

Baptism imprints on the soul an indelible spiritual sign, the character, which consecrates the Baptized person for Christian worship. Because of the character, Baptism cannot be repeated.

page 357, paragraph 1280

There simply is no mention of any such sign that

is associated with baptism in the Bible. The only sign or seal is the Holy Spirit in the believer until the day of redemption.

✝

Since the earliest times, Baptism has been administered to children (for it is a grace and a gift of God that does not presuppose any human merit). Children are baptized in the faith of the church. Entry into Christian life gives access to true freedom.

page 357, paragraph 1282

As I said earlier, there is no mention of infants or children being baptized in the Bible. The authors say, "For it is a grace and a gift of God." They are actually quoting from Eph 2:8 which says, "For by grace you have been saved through faith, and that not of yourselves; it is the gift of God." Notice, the authors leave out "by grace through faith." One should be very concerned when you see this kind of blatant changing of the Scripture. They take the gift of God and change it into a work that they perform through baptism! I say blatant because they not only change *by grace* to *a grace, the gift* to *a gift,* they completely leave out the words *you have been saved through faith.* It would appear that the authors would rather have you trusting in their church and the works they perform, as opposed to trusting in the true and living God! Also notice Eph 2:8 says, "you have been saved." This would mean that our salvation is complete when you place your faith in Christ. This leaves no room for praying for someone who has died in Christ. Faith in Christ gives access to him and true freedom.

✝

Baptism, the Eucharist, and the sacrament of confirmation together constitute the "sacraments of Christian initiation," whole unity must be safeguarded. It must be explained to the faithful that the reception of the sacrament of Confirmation is necessary for the completion of Baptismal grace. For by the sacrament of Confirmation, the Baptized are more perfectly bound to the Church and are enriched with a special strength of the Holy Spirit.

page 358, paragraph 1285

None of these things have anything to do with becoming a Christian. Remember, Eph 2:8 says, "For by grace you have been saved through faith, and that not of yourselves; it is the gift of God." There is no baptism, Eucharist or sacrament of confirmation that constitutes any Christian initiation. If you want to know you are in Christ, repent of your sin, and Jesus will be faithful and just to forgive you. First John 1:9 says, "If we confess our sins, He is faithful and just to forgive us our sins and to cleanse us from all unrighteousness." Moving ahead, it would appear that in order for a person to really be saved, according to the authors, one must have been baptized and confirmed in order for the baptismal grace or salvation to be complete. All that is really being done here is that men are taking the things that have association with God and then trying to make them a necessity in order to have access to God. This practice is not uncommon now and was not uncommon when Jesus was here on earth. The Pharisees had all kinds of rituals and practices of which meant nothing in the eyes of God because he is and was always interested in the heart that comes to him with a sincere faith. If your heart is not right with God, you are simply going through the motions of someone who is either pleasing themselves or men. I think it is an interesting choice of words when they say, "are more perfectly bound to the Church." Our goal as Christians is not to be more perfectly bound to other sinful people but to be more perfectly bound and transformed into the image of Christ our Lord. Don't misunderstand me; as believers in Christ, we should share a common unity in Christ's spirit, but we are not striving to be bound to anything other than Christ himself! Being enriched with a special strength of the Holy Spirit only happens when someone is born of the Spirit and spends time in God's Word, praying and fasting.

†

Confirmation perfects Baptismal grace; it is the sacrament which gives the Holy Spirit in order to root us more deeply in the divine filiation,

page 367, paragraph 1316

This kind of talk about the Holy Spirit would make it sound as though you were going to the doctor's office and he might administer the Holy Spirit to you as a prescription. The only problem is that the Holy Spirit administrates the Spirit on whomever he wills, not whomever man wills. My point being, unless the Spirit reveals himself to you and you are convicted of your sin, then and only then will the Holy Spirit be imparted to you. The gift of the Holy Spirit is the free gift of God and administered by him. Romans 8:8–11 says,

> So then, those who are in the flesh cannot please God. But you are not in the flesh but in the Spirit, if indeed the Spirit of God dwells in you. Now if anyone does not have the Spirit of Christ, he is not His. And if Christ is in you, the body is dead because of sin, but the Spirit is life because of righteousness. But if the Spirit of Him who raised Jesus from the dead dwells in you, He who raised Christ from the dead will also give life to your mortal bodies through His Spirit who dwells in you.

People should pray for others to come to the saving knowledge of Christ, but a man can never impart the Holy Spirit to another person.

†

The holy Eucharist completes Christian initiation. Those who have been raised to the dignity of royal priest hood by Baptism and configured more deeply to Christ by confirmation participate with the whole community in the LORD*'s own sacrifice by means of the Eucharist.*

page 368, paragraph 1322

Faith in Christ completes the Christian. Here again, you have all of these things being suggested to you, as if you need them in order to be complete in Christ, when in fact, it is our faith which as already completed us in him. By all of these actions, you would be trusting in the work of men's hands for your completion in God. If our God's power does not reach further than the works of the Catholic Church or any other church, then we had better find a more powerful God to serve. God is mighty to save and he is not in need of our assistance in so far as salvation is concerned! Trusting in the works of men will be of no added benefit when the LORD comes to gather those whom he foreknew from the foundation of the world. Furthermore, I hate to be the bearer of bad news, but no one can participate in the LORD's own sacrifice, for it is a finished work. He completed it once and for all. Hebrews 7:27 says, "Who does not need daily, as those high priests, to offer up sacrifices, first for His own sins and then for the people's, for this He did once for all when He offered up Himself."

Hebrews 8:1–2 says, "Now this is the main point of the things we are saying: We have such a High Priest, who is seated at the right hand of the throne of the Majesty in the heavens, a Minister of the sanctuary and of the true tabernacle which the LORD erected, and not man."

†

At the last supper, on the night he was betrayed, our savior instituted the Eucharistic sacrifice of His body and blood. This he did in order to perpetuate the sacrifice of the cross throughout the ages until he should come again, and so to entrust his beloved Spouse, the Church, a memorial of his death and resurrection: a sacrament of love, a sign of unity, a bond of charity, a paschal banquet in which Christ is consumed, the mind is filled with grace, and a pledge of future glory is given to us.

page 368, paragraph 1323

If this first sentence is true, and it is not, then the LORD and all the disciples were cannibals. Let's take a look at the Word as it pertains to communion. John says,

Jesus answered them and said, "Most assuredly, I say to you, you seek Me, not because you saw the signs, but because you ate of the loaves and were filled. Do not labor for the food which perishes, but for the food which endures to everlasting life, which the Son of Man will give you, because God the Father has set His seal on Him." Then they said to Him, "What shall we do, that we may work the works of God?" Jesus answered and said to them, "This is the work of God, that you believe in Him whom He sent." Therefore they said to Him, "What sign will You perform then, that we may see it and believe You? What work will You do? Our fathers ate manna in the desert; as it is written, 'He gave them bread from heaven to eat.'" Then Jesus said to them, "Most assuredly, I say to you, Moses did the not give you the bread from heaven, but My father gives you the true bread from heaven. For the bread of God is He who comes down from heaven and gives life to the world." Then they said to Him, "LORD, give us this bread always." And Jesus said to them, "I am the bread of life. He who comes to Me shall never hunger, and he who believes in Me shall never thirst. But I said to you that you have seen Me and yet do not believe. All that the Father gives Me will come to Me, and the one who comes to Me I will by no means cast out. For I have come down from heaven, not to do My own will, but the will of Him who sent Me. This is the will of the Father who sent Me, that all He has given Me I should lose nothing, but should raise it up at the last day. And this is the will of Him who sent Me, that everyone who sees the Son and believes in Him may have everlasting life; and I will raise him up at the last day." The Jews then murmured against Him, because He said, "I am the bread which came down from

> heaven." And they said, "Is not this Jesus the son of Joseph, whose Father and mother we know? How is it then that He says, 'I have come down from heaven'"? Jesus therefore answered and said to them, "Do not murmur among yourselves. No one can come to Me unless the Father who sent Me draws Him; and I will raise him up at the last day. It is written in the prophets, and they shall all be taught by God. Therefore everyone who has heard and learned from the Father comes to Me. Not that anyone has seen the Father, except He who is from God; He has seen the Father. Most assuredly, I say to you, he who believes in Me has everlasting life. I am the bread of life. Your fathers ate manna in the wilderness, and are dead. This is the bread which comes down from heaven, that one may eat of it and not die. I am the living bread which came down from heaven. If anyone eats of this bread, he will live forever; and the bread that I shall give is My flesh which I shall give for the life of the world." The Jews therefore quarreled among themselves, saying, "How can this man give us His flesh to eat?" Then Jesus said to them, "Most assuredly, I say to you, unless you eat the flesh of the Son of Man and drink His blood, you have no life in you. Whoever eats My flesh and drinks My blood has eternal life, and I will raise him at the last day. For My flesh is food indeed, and My blood is drink indeed. He who eats My flesh and drinks My blood abides in Me, and I in him. As the living Father sent Me, and I live because of the Father, so he who feeds on Me will live because of Me."
>
> John 6:26–66

When reading these verses, you must remember who Jesus said he is in John 1:14: "And the Word became flesh and dwelt among us, and we beheld His glory, the glory as of the begotten of the Father, full of grace and truth." You are fed by the, "pure milk of the word, that you may grow thereby" (1 Peter 2:1).

> This is the bread which came down from heaven—not as your fathers ate the manna, and are dead. He who eats this bread will live forever." These things He said in the synagogue as He taught in Capernaum. Therefore, many of His disciples, when they heard this, said, "This is a hard saying; who can understand it?" When Jesus knew in Himself that His disciples murmured about this, He said to them "Does this offend you? What then if you should see the Son of Man ascend where He was before? It is the Spirit who gives Life; the flesh profits nothing. The words that I speak to you are Spirit, and they are life. But there are some of you who do not believe." For Jesus knew from the beginning who would betray Him. And He said, "Therefore, I have said to you that no one can come to Me unless it has been granted to him by My Father." From that time many of his disciples went back and walked with Him no more.
>
> John 6:58–66

It is important to note that the disciples and the Jews were upset by the LORD saying that you must eat his flesh and drink his blood, but most people do not read, or listen as it were then, to the whole counsel of God. The LORD then goes on to say, "It is the Spirit who gives life; the flesh profits nothing. The words that I speak to you are Spirit, and they are life." Luke 22:19–20 says,

> And He took bread, gave thanks and broke it, and gave it to them, saying, "This is My body which is given for you; do this in remembrance of Me." Likewise He also took the cup after supper, saying, "This cup is the new covenant in My blood, which is shed for you."

Notice, the LORD says, "Do this in remembrance of Me." I am certain he was speaking about us remembering what he was about to go through on the cross. You must remember that unless the LORD shed his blood on the cross, there would be no remission of our sins. Matthew 26:28 says, "For this is My blood of the new covenant, which is shed for many for the remission of sins." The question one has to ask here was Christ's blood shed yet? No, because he had not gone to the cross yet. The LORD was speaking figuratively, trying to get his disciples to understand what he must do in order to redeem mankind. Furthermore, if it is the Spirit which gives life, then why would you need some physical Jesus in you as well? Galatians 2:19–21 says,

> For I through the law died to the law that I might live to God. I have been crucified with Christ; it is no longer I who live, but Christ lives in me; and the life which I now live in the flesh I live by faith in the Son of God, who loved Me and gave Himself for me. I do not set aside the grace of God; for if righteousness comes through the law, then Christ died in vain.

Paul was not suggesting that Christ lived in him because he had partaken of the Eucharist. Rather, he knew that the spirit of God lived in him because he had faith in the Son of God! Galatians 3:2–3 says,

> This only I want to learn from you: did you receive the Spirit by the works of the law, or by the hearing of faith? Are you so foolish? Having begun in the Spirit, are you now being made perfect by the flesh?

What is relevant to these verses and the Eucharist? Paul is saying that no one has ever received the Spirit by the works of men's hands, whether it is the Eucharist or some other practice.

Moving ahead in the paragraph, the authors say, "This He did in order to perpetuate the sacrifice of the cross throughout the ages until He should come again, and so to entrust to His beloved spouse, the church; a memorial of His death and resurrection." You cannot perpetuate the sacrifice of the cross and still have it as a memorial. Here we have a case of "double speak." By Webster's definition of *perpetuate* or *perpetual:* 1) be culpable, lasting forever, unceasing; 2) continuing without interruption, constant. You cannot have the LORD's death on the cross as both perpetual and a memorial at the same time. *Memorial* is defined by Webster as, "something, especially a monument, designed or established to perpetuate remembrance as of a person." Serving to perpetuate remembrance. This is extremely compelling evidence of the argument I made earlier that the LORD was and is trying to get his disciples—a person who believes in and helps disseminate the teachings of a master—to understand that it was and is by his shedding of blood at the cross and our receiving of his redemptive act that we actually are receiving him in faith, not physically. Going back to this idea that Christ's sacrifice is somehow perpetuated throughout the ages is completely against what the Word of God teaches. Hebrews 7:25–27 says,

> Therefore He is also able to save to the uttermost those who come to God through Him, since He ever lives to make intercession for them. For such a High Priest was fitting for us, who is holy, harmless, undefiled, separate from sinners, and has become higher than the heavens; who does not need daily, as those high priests, to offer up sacrifices, first for his own sins and then for the people's, for this He did once for all when He offered up Himself.

Note that the LORD says, "He ever lives to make intercession for them." He does not say the priest, Mary, or the saints live to make intercession for them. Also, He says he offered himself once; this does not mean twice or daily as it would be in the Eucharistic sacrifice. Once simply means once or one time. Christ could not have cried out, "It is finished," if there was to remain a perpetual sacrifice which would somehow aid in the remission of sins. John 19:30 says, "So when Jesus had received the sour wine, he said, 'It is finished!' And bowing his head, he gave up his spirit." Now then, is what the LORD did on the cross finished, or are we perpetuating it throughout the ages in the form of the Eucharist, or are we remembering it and giving thanks to God for what he did once and for all? Lastly, the authors say, "Christ is consumed." If this is true, and it is not, by what power or authority does the Catholic Church alone believe it can call the God of heaven and earth back into a wafer and wine?

Do you really suppose the God of the universe, who already humbled himself once and became flesh and blood, would then go to be glorified with his Father in heaven and then be called back out of heaven into a cup and a wafer, as if this would be of some spiritual benefit to us? I think not! When Christ returns for his bride, he will return in his glorified state, not as something fashioned by the works of men's hands!

✝

The Eucharist is the efficacious sign and sublime cause of that communion in the divine life and that unity of the People of God by which the Church is kept in being.

page 369, paragraph 1325

Here again, are we trusting in the Spirit or the works of men's hands for communion with God and the unity of the people of God by which the church is kept in being?

✝

In brief, the Eucharist is the sum and summary of our faith: "our way of thinking is attuned to the Eucharist, and the Eucharist in turn confirms our way of thinking."

page 369, paragraph 1327

In brief, our faith in the Spirit is the sum and summary of our faith: "our way of thinking is attuned to the Spirit, and the word in turn confirms our way of thinking."

†

The Holy Sacrifice, because it makes present the one sacrifice of Christ the savior and includes the Church's offering. The terms Holy Sacrifice are also used, since it completes and surpasses all the sacrifices of the old covenant.

page 370, paragraph 1330

We can never add to the sacrifice of which Christ laid down his life for our remission of sins. Furthermore, either we are trusting in his finished work on the cross, which completes us, or we are trusting in the works of men's hands, which can never complete us.

†

Holy Communion, because by this sacrament we unite ourselves to Christ, who makes us sharers in his body and blood to form a single body.

page 370, paragraph 1331

By faith in Christ we unite ourselves to Christ and become his ambassadors or his hands and feet on earth.

†

The Eucharistic sacrifice is also offered for the faithful departed who "have died in Christ but are not yet wholly purified," so that they may be able to enter into the light and peace of Christ:

page 382, paragraph 1371

Hebrews 10:1–18 says,

> For the law, having a shadow of the good things to come, and not the very image of the things, can never with these same sacrifices, which they offer continually year by year, make those who approach perfect. For then would they not have ceased to be offered? For the worshipers, once purged, would have had no more consciousness of sins. But in these sacrifices there is a reminder of sins every year. For it is not possible that the blood of bulls and goats could take away sins. Therefore, when He came into the world, He said: "Sacrifice and offering you did not desire, but a body you have prepared for Me. In burnt offering and sacrifices for sin you had no pleasure." Then I said, 'Behold, I have come in the volume of the book it is written of me to do your will, O God.'" Previously saying, "Sacrifice and offering, burnt offerings, and offerings for sin you did not desire, nor had pleasure in them" (which are offered according to the law) then He said, "Behold I have come to do your will, O God." He takes away the first that he may establish the second. By that will we have been sanctified through the offering of the body of Jesus Christ once for all. And every priest stands ministering daily and offering repeatedly the same sacrifices which can never take away sins. But this man, after He had offered one sacrifice for sins forever,

> sat down at the right hand of God, from that time waiting till His enemies are made His footstool. For by one offering He has perfected forever those who are being sanctified. And the Holy Spirit also witnesses to us; for after He had said before, "This is the covenant that I will make with them after those days, says the LORD: I will put my laws into their hearts, and in their minds I will write them," then He adds, "Their sins and their lawless deeds I will remember no more." Now where there is remission of these, there is no longer an offering for sin.

Now then, if we have been sanctified through the offering of the LORD's body on the cross, and having faith in his work on the cross, then how is it that the authors would suggest that we who are in Christ are not yet wholly purified? Clearly the Word says we have been sanctified. Furthermore, the LORD says he has perfected us forever and there is no longer an offering for sin. So, is what the LORD said true, or are we to trust in the offering of men's hands to aid us in his finished work? It is very important to note God says he offered one sacrifice, not a series of sacrifices or a perpetual sacrifice as it would be according to the authors of the catechism. Lastly, we are instructed not to offer sacrifices to the dead least we provoke the LORD to anger. Psalm 106:28–29 says, "And ate sacrifices made to the dead. Thus they provoked Him to anger with their deeds."

✝

It is highly fitting that Christ should have wanted to remain present to his church in this unique way. Since Christ was about to take his departure from his own in his visible form, he wanted to give us his sacramental presence; since he was about to offer himself on the cross to save us, he wanted us to have the memorial of love with which he loved us "to the end," even to the giving of his life. In his Eucharistic presence he remains mysteriously in our midst as the one who loved us and gave himself up for us, and he remains under signs that express and communicate this love: The Church and the world have a great need for Eucharistic worship. Jesus awaits us in this sacrament of love. Let us not refuse the time to go to meet him in adoration, in contemplation full of faith, and open to making amends for the serious offenses and crimes of the world. Let our adoration never cease.

page 385, paragraph 1380

The unique way in which Christ wanted to remain present to his church was and is through his Spirit. God seeks those who will worship him in spirit and truth.

✝

Holy Communion separates us from sin. The body of Christ we receive in Holy Communion is "given up for us," and the blood we drink "shed for the many for the forgiveness for sins. For this reason the Eucharist cannot unite us to Christ without at the same time cleansing us from past sins and preserving us from future sins: For as often as we eat this bread and drink the cup, we proclaim the death of the LORD. *If we proclaim the* LORD*'s death, we proclaim the forgiveness of sins. If, as often as his blood is poured out, it is poured for the forgiveness of sins, I should always receive* *it, so that it may always forgive my sins. Because I always sin, I should always have a remedy.*

page 390, paragraph 1393

Faith in Christ separates us from sin. For this reason, the Eucharist cannot unite us to Christ. Faith in Christ cleanses us from future sins. The second to last sentence says, "as often as His blood is poured out." His blood was poured out once for the forgiveness of sins! Hebrews 7:25–27 says,

> Therefore He is also able to save to the uttermost those who come to God through Him, since He ever lives to make intercession for them. For such a High Priest was fitting for us, who is holy, harmless, undefiled, separate form sinners, and has become higher than the heavens; who does not need daily, as those high priests, to offer up sacrifices, first for his own sins and then for the people's, for this He did once for all when He offered up Himself.

Hebrews 10:10–14 says,

> By that will we have been sanctified through the offering of the body of Jesus Christ once for all. And every priest stands ministering daily and offering repeatedly the same sacrifices, which can never take away sins. But this Man after He had offered one sacrifice for sins forever, sat down at the right hand of God, from that time waiting till his enemies are made his footstool. For by one offering He has perfected forever those who are being sanctified.

The great thing about these verses in Hebrews is that they make it clear that we always have a remedy for our sins because Christ forever lives to make intercession for us.

✝

By the same charity that it enkindles in us, the Eucharist preserves us from future mortal sins.

page 390, paragraph 1395

The Holy Spirit preserves us from future sins. If we will confess them to Jesus, he is faithful and just to forgive us.

✝

It is Christ Himself, the eternal high priest of the new covenant who, acting through the ministry of the priests, offers the Eucharistic sacrifice. And it is the same Christ, really present under the species of bread and wine, who is the offering of the Eucharistic sacrifice.

page 394, paragraph 1410

Once again, it is made clear in the previous verses listed in Hebrews that Christ offered himself once on the cross, and there is no need of priests to aid him in performing more sacrifices which cannot take away sin!

✝

Only validly ordained priests can preside at the Eucharist and consecrate the bread and the wine, so that they become the body and blood of the LORD.

page 394, paragraph 1411

Do you think Christ would exclude the rest of the believing church, who have come to him by faith in his finished work on the cross? What is interesting about this paragraph is that once again the believer is in need of an ordained priest in order to participate in communion. Yet, I don't see this model in the New Testament church, nor do I see it in the rest of the believing church today.

✝

It is called the sacrament of confession of sins to a priest is an essential element of this sacrament. In a profound sense it is also a "confession"—acknowledgment and praise—of the holiness of God and of his mercy toward sinful man. It is called the sacrament of forgiveness, since by the priest's sacramental absolution God grants the penitent "pardon and peace."

page 397, paragraph 1424

As stated previously, why would you go to a sinful man when you can go directly to a righteous and holy God, who forever lives to make intercession for us? No man can forgive another man of his sins; only Christ can, who died once and for all of our sins! Webster defines *absolution* as "formal remission of sin imparted by a priest." The only problem with this theory is that it is a direct contradiction to the Word of God. The only High Priest who has a rite of absolution is Jesus Christ! You see, Christ is still the High Priest of his church; there has never been a transfer of who died for sins and forgives us.

✝

The interior penance of the Christian can be expressed in many and various ways. Scripture and the fathers insist above all on three forms, fasting, prayer, and almsgiving, which express conversion in relation to oneself, to God, and to others.

page 400, paragraph 1434

The interior penance of the Christian can be expressed in many and various ways. Scripture and the fathers insist above all on three forms—fasting, prayer, and almsgiving—which express conversion in relation to oneself, to God, and to others. Alongside the radical purification brought about by baptism or martyrdom they cite as means of obtaining forgiveness of sins: efforts at reconciliation with one's neighbor, tears of repentance, concern for the salvation of one's neighbor, the intercession of the saints, and the practice of charity, "which covers a multitude of sins." Webster defines penance as "a voluntary act of devotion or self-mortification to show sorrow for sin or misdeed," a sacrament that consists of contrition, confession, acceptance of punishment imposed by the confessor, and absolution. The only true *penance,* for a lack of a better word, is repentance or a turning away form one's sins. God does not impose a direct punishment for our sins, except that Christ bore all our sins on the cross. He bore our sins so we don't have to pay the penalty for them. Our sins still have a negative effect on us and on the lives of those around us, but God is faithful and just to forgive our sins, if we will confess them to him! Baptism or martyrdom is never cited as a means for the forgiveness of sins. These two and efforts at reconciliation with one's neighbor, tears of repentance, concern for the salvation of one's neighbor, and the practice of charity are cited as natural byproducts of a person who has been forgiven of their sins. You will not find any case in the Bible where a dead believer or saint, as the authors call such a person, is making intercession for a person's forgiveness of sin. For there is one mediator between God and man; that man is the LORD Jesus Christ! See 1 Tim 2:5.

✝

Eucharist and penance. Daily conversion and penance find their source and nourishment in the Eucharist, For in it is made present the sacrifice of Christ which has reconciled us with God. Through the Eucharist those who live from the life of Christ are fed and strengthened. It is a remedy to free us from our daily faults and to preserve us from mortal sins.

page 400, paragraph 1436

We are daily being transformed into the image of Christ, as we daily walk with him, through the power of the Holy Spirit, which resides in the believer. There is no need to remake the sacrifice which Christ already made, which for those who believe through faith have already been reconciled with God! Faith in Christ is the remedy to free us from all our sins past, present and future.

✝

Since he is the Son of God, Jesus says of himself, "the Son of man has authority on earth to forgive sins" and exercises the divine power: "your sins are forgiven." Only God forgives sins. By virtue of his divine authority he gives this power to men to exercise in his name.

page 402, paragraph 1441

This paragraph starts where it should finish! I don't know how the authors can make a statement like this and still say you should confess your sins to a priest, pray to the saints, pray to Mary, and do all the various other works, which can never forgive a person of their sins! Furthermore, you never see a biblical account of a man forgiving another man of his sins. Otherwise, the authors would have cited it and would have some basis for the practices of which they preach.

✝

I will give you the keys of the kingdom of heaven, and whatever you bind on earth shall be bound in heaven and whatever you loose on earth shall be loosed in heaven. The office of binding and loosing which was given to Peter was also assigned to the college of the apostles united to its head.

page 402, paragraph 1444

This verse is from Matthew 18:18–19, which says,

> Assuredly, I say to you, whatever you bind on earth will be bound in heaven and whatever you loose on earth will be loosed in heaven. "Again I say to you that if two of you agree on earth concerning anything that they ask, it will be done for them by My Father in heaven.

Notice, there is no mention of the office of binding and loosing being given to Peter. Rather, this gift of prayer is for every believer in Christ that we might have an impact in the world in which we live.

✝

The words bind and loose mean: whomever you exclude from your communion, will be excluded from communion with God; whomever you receive anew into your communion, God will welcome back into his. Reconciliation with the Church is inseparable from reconciliation with God.

page 403, paragraph 1445

Once again, you find the authors limiting God's power to save by saying, "The Church is inseparable from reconciliation with God." Sure, God has chosen those who are born of his spirit to be instruments of reconciliation by proclaiming his redemptive power. But, if we don't proclaim his truth to the unbelieving world, he is not limited by what we do or don't do. God will still save all who he has chosen from the foundation of the world.

✝

Over the centuries the concrete form in which the Church has exercised this power received from the LORD *has varied considerably. During the first centuries the reconciliation of Christians who had committed particularly grave sins after their Baptism (for example, idolatry, murder, or adultery) was tied to a very rigorous discipline, according to which penitents had to do public penance for their sins, often for years, before receiving reconciliation. To this "order of penitents" (which concerned only certain regions only once in a lifetime. During the seventh century Irish missionaries, inspired by the eastern monastic tradition, took to continental Europe the "private" practice of penance, which does not require public and prolonged completion of penitential works before reconciliation with the Church. From that time on, the sacrament has been performed in secret between penitent and priest. This new practice envisioned the possibility of repetition and so opened the way to a regular frequenting of this sacrament. It allowed the forgiveness of grave sins and venial sins and venial sins to be integrated into one sacramental celebration. In its main lines this is the form of penance that the Church has practiced down to our day.*

page 403, paragraph 1447

Although the Catholic Church has varied considerably on the issue of forgiveness of sins, God has not! Malachi 3:6 says, "For I am the LORD, I do not change." There is a great example of how Jesus forgives us of our sins without any confession to a priest or penance. John 8:3–11 says,

> Then the scribes and Pharisees brought to Him a woman caught in adultery. And when they had

> set her in the midst, they said to Him, "Teacher, this woman was caught in adultery, in the very act. Now Moses, in the law, commanded us that such be stoned. But what do you say?" This they said, testing Him, that they might have something of which to accuse Him. But Jesus stooped down and wrote on the ground with His finger, as though He did not hear. So when they continued asking Him, he raised Himself up and said to them, "He who is without sin among you, let him throw a stone at her first." And again He stooped down and wrote on the ground. Then those who heard it, being convicted by their conscience, went out one by one, beginning with the oldest even to the last. And Jesus was left alone, and the woman standing in the midst. When Jesus had raised Himself up and saw no one but the woman, He said to her, "Woman, where are those accusers of yours? Has no one condemned you?" She said, "No one, Lord." And Jesus said to her, "Neither do I condemn you; go and sin no more."

These verses illustrate the wonderful redemptive power of Christ alone! Jesus knew that the Pharisees and all men and women are not without sin. That is why Jesus was left alone and the woman was standing in his midst. The same is true of you and I; we are left all alone in our sins, except Jesus is standing there waiting, willing and able to forgive us if we will confess our sin and turn from it. Jesus planned for us to have direct access to him by laying down his life on the cross. It would be a grave sin to go to any of his created sinful people rather than him who bore our sins so we can say *Abba*, or Father.

†

The Church, who through the bishop and his priests forgives sins in the name of Jesus Christ and determines the manner of satisfaction, also prays for the sinner and does penance with him. Thus the sinner is healed and re-established in ecclesial communion.

page 404, paragraph 1448

As previously stated, no man can forgive another man's sins, and why would another sinful human think he had a rite to determine another sinners manner of satisfaction for the sin? Christ has already determined the manner of satisfaction for forgiveness of sin: confess and repent.

†

The formula of absolution used in the Latin Church expresses the essential elements of this sacrament: the Father of mercies is the source of all forgiveness.

page 404, paragraph 1449

Just the wording here should sound a spiritual alarm. There is no formula by which a man can forgive another man's sins. This type of thinking gets us into trusting in the work of sinful men rather than a sinless God who lives forever to make intercession for his saints. Jesus is the source by which all forgiveness flows, for he alone has purchased us by the shedding of his blood.

†

When it arises from a love by which God is loved above all else, contrition is called "perfect." (Contrition of charity.) Such contrition remits venial sins: it also obtains forgiveness of mortal sins if it includes the firm resolution to have recourse to sacramental confession as soon as possible.

page 405, paragraph 1452

I'm afraid that this type of teaching is leading many people to trust in their own abilities, or the abilities of another person, when all anyone has to do is put their trust in the LORD Jesus, who is faithful and just to forgive us of all our sins! You know, it would be one thing if you could find the formula of absolution in the Bible or sacramental confession, but you cannot, and I am so thankful that his ways are not like our ways. Otherwise, I would always be wondering if I had done enough to undo my sin. But, with Jesus as my savior and his spirit living in me, all I have to do is trust and believe in all his wonderful promises, which are based on his faithfulness and goodness, not on my limited resources.

†

By itself however, imperfect contrition cannot obtain the forgiveness of grave sins, but it disposes one to obtain forgiveness in the sacrament of penance.

page 405, paragraph 1453

My response is the same as paragraph 1452.

†

Confession to a priest is an essential part of the sacrament of penance.

page 405, paragraph 1456

For there is one mediator between God and man, and that man is the Lord Jesus Christ. Hebrews 7:22–28 says,

> By so much more Jesus has become a surety of a better covenant. And there were many priests, because they were prevented by death from continuing, but because He continues forever, has an unchangeable priesthood. Therefore He is also able to save to the uttermost those who come to God through Him, since he ever lives to make intercession for them. For such a High Priest was fitting for us, who is holy, harmless, undefiled separate form sinners and has become higher than the heavens, who does not need daily, as those high priests, to offer up sacrifices, first for His own sins and then for the people's, for this He did once for all when he offered up himself. For the law appoints as high priest men who have weakness, but the word of the oath, which came after the law, appoints the Son who has been perfected forever.

†

According to the Church's command, "after having the age of discretion, each of the faithful is bound by an obligation faithfully to confess serious sins at least once a year. Anyone who is aware of having committed a mortal sin must not receive Holy Communion, even if he experiences deep contrition, without having first received sacramental absolution, unless he has a grave reason for receiving communion and there is no possibility of going to confession. Children must go to the sacrament of penance before receiving Holy Communion for the first time."

page 406, paragraph 1457

I'm not sure where they have come up with the idea of confessing their sins at least once a year, but God would have us to daily confess our sins, and he is faithful and just to forgive us. David gives us an example of how we are to pray in Psalm 26:2–5:

> Examine me, O LORD, and prove me; try my mind and my heart. For your loving kindness is before my eyes, and I have walked in your truth. I have not sat with idolatrous mortals, nor will I go in with hypocrites. I have hated the congregation of evildoers, and will not sit with the wicked.

First Corinthians 11:24–31 says,

> And when He had given thanks, He broke it and said, "Take, eat; this is My body which is broken for you; do this in remembrance of Me." In the same manner He also took the cup after supper, saying, "This cup is the new covenant in My blood. This do, as often as you drink it, in remembrance of Me." For as often as you eat this bread and drink this cup, you

> proclaim the LORD's death until he comes. Therefore whoever eats this bread or drinks this cup of the LORD in an unworthy manner will be guilty of the body and blood of the LORD. But let a man examine himself, and so let him eat of that bread and drink of that cup, for he who eats and drinks in an unworthy manner eats and drinks judgment to himself, not discerning the LORD's body. For this reason many are weak and sick among you, and many sleep. For if we would judge ourselves, we would not judged.

There are a few key points revealed in these verses. First, the LORD says, "This is my body which is broken you." Had the LORD's body been broken yet? No, because he had not gone to the cross. He was trying to get them to understand the price he would pay with his body and his shedding of his blood. So, did the LORD break off a piece of his body and pour out his blood in the cup while he was there with them, or was he speaking figuratively of the things which were going to take place? Second Corinthians 13:4–5 says,

> "For though He was crucified in weakness, yet He lives by the power of God. For we also are weak in Him, but we shall live with Him by the power of God toward you. Examine yourselves as to whether you are in the faith. Prove yourselves, do you not know yourselves, that Jesus Christ is in you? Unless, indeed, you are disqualified."

It is also apparent by these verses that we are to examine ourselves in relationship to Jesus and his Word. If we stay in his Word and walk in his ways, we will never have worry about adhering to a church's set of beliefs because our feet will be firmly planted on the Rock.

✝

Without being strictly necessary, confession of everyday faults (venial sins) is nevertheless strongly recommended by the Church. Indeed the regular confession of our venial sins helps us form our conscience, fight against evil tendencies, let ourselves be healed by Christ and progress in the life of the spirit. By receiving more frequently through this sacrament the gift of the father's mercy, we are spurred to be merciful as he is merciful.

page 406, paragraph 1458

Here again, we must remember that he wants us to confess all sin to him so that nothing will hinder us form being conformed into his image.

✝

Absolution takes away sin, but it does not remedy all the disorders sin has caused. Raised up from sin, the sinner must still recover his full spiritual health by doing something more to make amends for the sin: He must "make satisfaction for" or "expiate" his sin: This satisfaction is also called "penance."

page 407, paragraph 1459

To fully understand this paragraph, we must first define absolution, expiate, and penance. *Absolution* is the formal remission of sin imparted by a priest. *Expiation* is to make amends for or atone for some wrongdoing. *Penance* is a voluntary act of devotion or self-mortification to show sorrow for a sin or misdeed; a sacrament that consists of contrition, confession, acceptance of punishment imposed by the confessor, and absolution. No one can absolve another person's sin expect for Christ alone. There is nothing more or less a person can do except confess his or her sin to Jesus and repent. Christ has already made amends for all our sins past, present, and future; our only responsibility is to confess and repent of them. *Repentance* is to feel regret or remorse; to resolve to reform one self morally. The very act of repenting shows God that we realize the error of our sin so that he can restore us by the power of his spirit. To suggest that we should have to perform some act of penance would also suggest that his finished work on the cross for all of our sins would somehow not be sufficient for the absolution of all our sins. First John 1:9 says, "If we confess our sins, he is faithful and just to forgive us our sins and to cleanse us from all unrighteousness." And Romans 3:26–28 says, "that He might be just and the justifier of the one who has faith in Jesus. Where is boasting then? It is excluded. By what law? Of works? No, but by the law of faith. Therefore we conclude that a man is justified by faith apart from the deeds of the law."

✝

Such penances help configure us to Christ, who alone expiated our sins once for all. They allow us to become co-heirs with the risen Christ, "provided we suffer with him."

page 407, paragraph 1460

Our works or penances, as the authors refer to them, have nothing to do with conforming us into the image of Christ; works are simply a by-product of the spirit of God working in us and through us. Faith alone allows us to become coheirs with the risen Christ. Second Timothy 3:12–17 says,

> Yes, and all who desire to live godly in Christ Jesus will suffer persecution. But evil men and impostors will grow worse and worse, deceiving and being deceived. But as for you, continue in the things which you have learned and have been assured of, knowing from whom you have learned them, and that from childhood you have known the Holy Scriptures, which are able to make you wise for salvation through faith which is in Christ Jesus. All Scripture is given by inspiration of God, and is profitable for doctrine, for reproof, for correction, for instruction in righteousness, that the man of God may be complete, thoroughly equipped for every good work.

The Word of God assures us that we will suffer persecution for living godly in Christ Jesus, but you will not find our suffering having anything to do with becoming coheirs with the risen Christ. Here is an example. If you have had a child, the child is your son or daughter, whether or not the child is good or bad. When the child disobeys you, you often wish he or she were sorry for what they did, but whether or not they say their sorry, this does not negate the fact that they are still your child. Similarly, once you have asked Christ into your heart and to forgive you of our sins, you are a child of God. This fact has everything to do with our faith in who God is and what he did for us on the cross and nothing to do with whether or not we suffer as he did. Remember, he told us we suffer because of our association with him, rather than suffer so we would have a right to associate with him.

†

Indeed bishops and priests, by virtue of the sacrament of holy orders, have the power to forgive all sins "in the name of the Father, and the Son, and of the Holy Spirit."

page 408, paragraph 1461

This power to forgive all sins was given to Jesus alone. Pastors and priests are simply men who God will use to point people to the source of true redemption found in Jesus Christ alone.

†

Certain particularly grave sins incur excommunication, the most severe ecclesiastical penalty, which impedes the reception of the sacraments and the exercise of certain ecclesiastical acts, and for which absolution consequently cannot be granted, according to canon law, except by the pope, the bishop of the place or priests authorized by them. In danger any priest, even if deprived of faculties for hearing confessions, can absolve from every sin and excommunication.

page 408, paragraph 1463

We can thank God that he is not a man who is deprived of his faculties for hearing our confessions of sin but is the same today, yesterday, and forever. He is always ready and able to forgive anyone of any sin if we will simply come to him and ask for forgiveness. He is faithful and just to forgive us of all our sins.

†

The priest is the sign and the instrument of God's merciful love for the sinner.

page 409, paragraph 1465

Jesus is the sign and the instrument of God's merciful love for the sinner. As I said earlier, all believing men and women are to be instruments used by God to point the world to Jesus and his wonderful redemptive power, which can only be found in him.

†

For it is now, in this life, that we are offered the choice between life and death, and it is only by the road of conversion that we can enter the kingdom, from which one is excluded by grave sin. In converting to Christ through penance and faith, the sinner passes from death to life and "does not come into judgment."

page 410, paragraph 1470

You will not find any mention of anyone being excluded from the kingdom of God for having committed a supposedly grave sin. You will only find people outside the kingdom of God who rejected Jesus as being the only source of redemption for them and the sins they have committed. It is only by turning to Christ, through faith, that the sinner passes from death to life and "does not come into judgment." You see, if there were some penance we could perform to aid in our removal of sin, then God's Word would become void because God says, "But we are all like and unclean thing, and all our righteousnesses are like filthy rags" (Isaiah 64:6). When God looks on a person who has accepted his son's sacrifice on the cross for their sins, he no longer sees the sin, except that his son's blood covers their sin. Philippians 3:9 says, "And be found in Him, not having my own righteousness, which is from the law, but that which is through faith in Christ, the righteousness which is from God by faith."

✝

An indulgence is partial or plenary according as it removes either part or all of the temporal punishment due to sin. Indulgences may be applied to the living or the dead.

page 411, paragraph 1471

No man has the ability to remove either part or all of the temporal punishment due to sin. Sin by its very nature has consequences, which are damaging. One has to look no further than the many examples found throughout the Bible. Furthermore, you will not find anyone in the Bible having indulgences performed while they were living or dead. One can be sure that if you have not been born of the spirit of God by faith in this life, you will certainly face the judgment of God in the life to come. It will not matter if the entire church in the world was trying to pray you or indulge you into a right relationship with God; you will still face the judgment of God! Hebrews 9:27–28 says,

> And as it is appointed for men to die once, but after this the judgment, so Christ was offered once to bear the sins of many. To those who eagerly wait for Him He will appear a second time, apart from sin, for salvation.

Don't hope or trust in the abilities of another human being just like you and me, rather put your full trust in Christ who alone can save your soul from death and hell.

✝

To understand this doctrine and practice of the Church, it is necessary to understand that sin has a double consequence. Grave sin deprives us of communion with God and therefore makes us incapable of eternal life, the privation of which is called the "eternal punishment" of sin. On the other hand every sin, even venial, entails an unhealthy attachment to creatures, which must be purified either here on earth, or after death in the state called purgatory. This purification frees one from what is called the "temporal punishment" of sin. These two punishments must not be conceived of as kind of vengeance inflicted by God from without, but as following from the very nature of sin. A conversion which proceeds from a fervent charity can attain the complete purification of the sinner in such a way that no punishment would remain.

page 411, paragraph 1472

Any sin deprives us of communion with God and therefore must be dealt with by repenting of the sin so that we do not hinder our own spiritual growth. But, our sin in no way changes whether or not we are his children or not. Secondly, you will find no mention of a place in the Bible called purgatory. Simply think about your own children if you have them. If they are disobedient or sin, you do not take away their birthright. You may or should discipline them quickly for their actions, but their actions do not change the fact that they are still your children. Similarly, God knew from the foundations of the world that we would sin, but he still sees the faith we placed in his Son and his blood covers our sin if we will confess it to him. Look at Luke 16:26 which says, "And besides all this, between us and you there is a great gulf fixed, so that those who want to pass from here to you cannot, nor can those from there pass to us." To paraphrase this verse, Luke is telling us that there is no passing back and forth between heaven and hell. Lastly, the only conversion which can attain the complete purification of the sinner is placing your full trust in Jesus by faith alone. Herein lies the place of knowing there will be no punishment or judgment for those found in Christ Jesus and abiding in his Word.

✝

While patiently bearing sufferings and trails of all kinds and, when the day comes, serenely facing death, the Christian must strive to accept this temporal punishment of sin as a grace. He should strive (by works) of mercy and charity, as well as by prayer and various practices of penance, to put off completely the "old man" and to put on the "new man."

page 411, paragraph 1473

Romans 3:26–28 says,

> To demonstrate at the present time His righteousness, that He might be just and the justifier of the one who has faith in Jesus. Where is boasting then? It is excluded. By what law? Of works? No, but by the law of faith. Therefore we conclude that a man is justified by faith apart from the deeds of the law.

I think what the authors are missing in terms of our forgiveness of sin is that this is accomplished by the power of the spirit of God. Ephesians 4:20–24 says,

> But you have not so learned Christ, if indeed you have heard Him and have been taught by Him, as the truth is in Jesus: that you put off, concerning your former conduct the old man which grows corrupt according to the deceitful lusts, and be renewed in the spirit of your mind, and that you put on the new man which was created according to God, in righteousness and true holiness.

Romans 7: 4–6 says,

> Therefore, my brethren, you also have become dead to the law through the body of Christ, that you may be married to another, even to Him who was raised from the dead, that we should bear fruit to God. For when we were in the flesh, the passions of sins which were aroused by the law were at work in our members to bear fruit to death. But now we have been delivered from the law, having died to what we were held by, so that we should serve in the newness of the Spirit and not in the oldness of the letter.

Galatians 2:16–21 says,

> Knowing that a man is not justified by the works of the law but by faith in Jesus Christ, even we have believed in Christ Jesus. That we might be justified by faith in Christ and not by the works of the law; for by the works no flesh shall be justified. But if, while we seek to be justified by Christ, we ourselves also are found sinners, is Christ therefore a minister of sin? Certainly not! For if I build again

> those things which I destroyed, I make myself a transgressor, for I through the law died to the law that I might live to God. I have been crucified with Christ; it is no longer I who live, but Christ lives in me; and the life which I now live in the flesh I live by faith in the Son of God, who loved me and gave Himself for me. I do not set aside the grace of God; for if righteousness comes through the law, then Christ died in vain.

This last sentence pretty much sums up all the verses combined, in that, if our works could add to our righteousness, then Christ died in vain. Galatians 3:11–14 says,

> But that no one is justified by the law in the sight of God is evident, for "the just shall live by faith." Yet the law is not of faith, but "the man who does them shall live by them." Christ has redeemed us from the curse of the law, having become a curse for us (for it is written, "Cursed is everyone who hangs on a tree"), that the blessing of Abraham might come upon the Gentiles in Christ Jesus, that we might receive the promise of the Spirit through Faith.

Lastly, I believe Romans 4:1–9 puts a stop to any argument as to how one is forgiven for their sin.

> What then shall we say that Abraham our father has found according to the flesh? For if Abraham was justified by works, he has something of which to boast, but not before God, for what does the Scripture say? Abraham believed God, and it was accounted to him for righteousness, now to him who works, the wages are not counted as grace but as debt. But to him who does not work but believes on Him who justifies the ungodly, his faith

> is accounted for righteousness, just as David also describes the blessedness of the man to whom God imputes righteousness apart from works: "Blessed are those whose lawless deeds are forgiven, and whose sins are covered; blessed is the man to whom the LORD shall not impute sin. Does this blessedness then come upon the circumcised only, or upon the uncircumcised also? For we say that faith was accounted to Abraham for righteousness!"

You see, what is made clear in these verses is that Abraham, David, and every believer throughout history have never been justified by the works they have done. But, they were justified by their faith in God, the same way you and I are justified today. David had a blessed assurance that only comes by putting his trust in the living God. He was not relying on the works of his hands or the hands of any other man. He knew that all his lawless deeds were forgiven and all his sins were covered because he had placed his faith in the living God!

✝

The Christian who seeks to purify himself of his sin and to become holy with the help of God's grace is not alone.

page 412, paragraph 1474

This sentence clearly shows the authors' misunderstanding of how a person is purified from sin. The only help of being purified from our sins is through faith and the grace of God! To suggest that we might need God's help coupled with our works would also mean that Christ died in vain. If we could do something to remove our sin by our works, then Christ would not have been nailed to the cross.

✝

We also call these spiritual goods of the communion of saints the Church's treasury, which is not the sum total of the material goods which have accumulated during the course of the centuries. On the contrary the treasury of the Church is the infinite value, which can never be exhausted, which Christ's merits have before God. They were offered so that the whole of mankind could be set free from sin and attain communion with the Father.

page 412, paragraph 1476

Christ's action alone is the only thing that sets us free from sin, no matter what is in the church's treasury. Also, you must remember the church, from God's perspective, are those who are born of the spirit of God, not some building of global institution.

✝

This treasury includes as well the prayers and good works of the Blessed Virgin Mary. They are truly immense, unfathomable, and even pristine in their value before God. In the treasury, too, are the prayers and good works of all the saints, all those who have followed in the footsteps of Christ the LORD *and by his grace have made their lives holy and carried out the mission the Father entrusted to them. In this way they attained their own salvation and at the same time cooperated in saving their brothers in the unity of the mystical body.*

page 412, paragraph 1477

The only problem with this whole treasury theory is there is no basis for it found in the Bible. It is a nice thought to think Mary, David, Moses, or any of the men or women who lived a life of faith, which is why they are with the LORD in heaven, are praying for us. But, the truth of the matter is that they are not; we know this because the Bible tells us there is only one intercessor between God and man: Christ alone. You cannot afford to be misled into believing that other created human beings will somehow assist you in your acceptance before God. God will only ask you what you did with his Son, not Mary or any other person.

†

The Byzantine liturgy recognizes several formulas of absolution, in the form of invocation, which admirably express the mystery of forgiveness

page 413, paragraph 1481

The only biblical formula for absolution is by placing one's faith in Christ alone.

†

One who desires to obtain reconciliation with God and with the Church, must confess to a priest all the unconfessed grave sins he remembers after having carefully examined his conscience.

page 416, paragraph 1493

Once again, this is never found in the Bible.

†

Through indulgences the faithful can obtain the remission of temporal punishment resulting from sin for themselves and also for the souls in purgatory.

page 417, paragraph 1498

No work on our part can obtain the remission of temporal punishment resulting from sin or for souls who have passed on onto hell. I say hell because there is no place called purgatory found in the Bible.

†

Suffering, a consequence of original sin, acquires a new meaning; it becomes a participation in the saving work of Jesus.

page 423, paragraph 1521

Nothing we can offer becomes a participation in the saving work of Jesus! His saving work was done and completed when he died on the cross. Suffering and trials are simply a means by which God conforms us into the image of his Son.

†

The anointing of the sick completes our conformity to the death and resurrection of Christ, just as Baptism began it. It completes the holy anointings that make the whole Christian life: that of Baptism which sealed the new life in us, and that of confirmation which strengthened us for the combat of this life. This last anointing fortifies the end of our earthly life like a solid rampart for the final struggles before entering the Father's house.

page 424, paragraph 1523

The Holy Spirit completes our conformity to the death and resurrection of Christ, just as receiving the Holy Spirit began it. It is the Holy Spirit which sealed the new life in us. Ephesians 4:30 says, "And do not grieve the Holy Spirit of God, by whom you were sealed for the day of redemption." Second Corinthians 1:21–22 says, "Now He who establishes us with you in Christ and has anointed us is God. Who also has sealed us and given us the Spirit in our hearts as a deposit."

Lastly, there will be no final struggles before entering the Father's house. The Word of God is very clear as to what happens after we die. If you are a believer in Christ, you will go to the *bema* seat of Christ, and it is there our works will be tried by fire. Whatever works were done in the right spirit will last, and we will receive a reward. Whatever works were done in the flesh will be burned with fire. But in either case, these works have no bearing on our getting into heaven. Those who have not been born of his Spirit will face the judgment seat of Christ upon which they will hear, "Depart from Me, I never knew you."

†

In addition to the anointing of the sick, the Church offers those who are about to leave this life the Eucharist as Viaticum. Communion in the body and blood of Christ, received at this moment of "passing over" to the Father, has a particular significance and importance. It is the seed of eternal life and the power of resurrection, according to the words of the LORD*: "He who eats my flesh and drinks my blood has eternal life, and I will raise him up at the last day."*

page 424, paragraph 1524

There is no mention of taking communion or the Eucharist in the Bible as you are dying. Once again, if you were trusting in the work of the priest to change the elements into Christ's blood and body because you thought this would be of some help to your getting in heaven, then you would be mistaken. Remember, being born of the Spirit of God is the only thing that brings us into a right standing with God! Let's go back to John 6:54–66 because I believe it is very important to understand. In verse 61, Jesus says, "Does this offend you?" He knew that anyone would be offended at the suggestion of eating another person's body and drinking their blood. This is why you must read all of the Word of God in context. You cannot take a verse, especially a verse like this, and not check its meaning. You find the true meaning of the verse in verse 63: "It is the Spirit who gives life; the flesh profits nothing. The words that I speak to you are spirit, and they are life."

✝

Two other sacraments, Holy Orders and Matrimony, are directed towards the salvation of others; if they contribute as well to personal salvation, it is through service to others that they do so.

page 426, paragraph 1534

Once again our works or service to others has nothing to do with our being saved or not!

✝

The chosen people were constituted by God as "a kingdom of priests and a holy nation." But within the people of Israel, God chose one of the twelve tribes, that of Levi, and set it apart for liturgical service; god himself is its inheritance. A special rite consecrated the beginnings of the priesthood of the Old Covenant. The priests are "appointed to act on behalf of men in relation to God, to offer gifts and sacrifices for sins.

page 428, paragraph 1539

This is a true statement, but the authors failed to tell you that Christ also did away with the priesthood all together. Hebrews 8:13 says, "In that he says, 'A new covenant,' He has made the first obsolete. Now what is becoming obsolete and growing old is ready to vanish away." Then in Hebrews 9:11–15,

> But Christ came as High Priest of the good things to come, with the greater and more perfect tabernacle not made with hands, that is not of this creation. Not with the blood of goats and calves, but with His own blood He entered the most holy place once for all, having obtained eternal redemption. For if the blood of bulls and goats and the ashes of a heifer, sprinkling the unclean, sanctifies for the purifying of the flesh, how much more shall the blood of Christ, who through the eternal Spirit offered Himself without spot to God, purge your conscience from dead works to serve the living God? And for this reason He is the Mediator of the new covenant, by means of death, for the redemption of the transgressions under the first covenant, that those who are called may receive the promise of the eternal inheritance.

Lastly, Hebrews 7: 27–28 says,

> Who does not need daily, as those high priests, to offer up sacrifices, first for His own sins and then for the people's, for this He did once for all when he offered up Himself. For the law appoints as high priests men who have weakness, but the word of the oath, which came after the law, appoints the Son who has been perfected forever.

These verses show Christ having done away with the priesthood as we know it. But I would highly recommend reading Hebrews in its entirety and Hebrews chapter 7, 8, and 9 more specifically.

✝

The liturgy of the Church, however, sees in the priesthood of Aaron and the service of the Levites, as in the institution of the seventy elders, a prefiguring of the ordained ministry of the new covenant.

page 428, paragraph 1541

This is an interesting concept, expect it is in direct opposition to the Word of God. Hebrews 7:11–28 says,

> Therefore, if perfection were through the Levitical priesthood (for under it the people received the law), what further need was there that another priest should rise according to the order of Melchizedek, and not be called according to the order of Aaron? For the priesthood being changed of necessity there is also a change of the law. For He whom these things are spoken belongs to another tribe, from which no man has officiated at the altar. For it is evident that

> our Lord arose from Judah, of which tribe Moses spoke nothing concerning priesthood. And it is yet far more evident if, in the likeness of Melchizedek, there arises another priest who has come, not according to the law of a fleshly commandment, but according to the power of an endless life. For he testifies: "you are a priest forever according to the order of Melchizedek." For on the one hand there is an annulling of the former commandment because of its weakness and unprofitableness, for the law made nothing perfect; on the other hand, there is the bringing in of a better hope, through which we draw near to God. And inasmuch as He was not made priest without an oath (for they have become priests without an oath, but He with an oath by Him who said to Him: "the Lord has sworn and will not relent, 'You are a priest forever according to the order of Melchizdek'"), by so much more Jesus has become a surety of a better covenant. And there were many priests, because they were prevented by death from continuing. But He, because He continues forever, has an unchangeable priesthood. Therefore He is also able to save to the uttermost those who come to God through Him, since He lives to make intercession for them. For such a High Priest was fitting for us, who is holy, harmless, undefiled, separate form sinners, and has become higher than the heavens; who does not need daily, as those high priests, to offer up sacrifices, first for His own sins and then for the people's, for this He did once for all when He offered up Himself.

The ordained ministry found in the new testament is a chosen people of God, a royal priesthood of believers who sing our Lord's praises and declare his truth. It is not a group of men chosen by other men, who may or may not even be born of the Spirit of God.

†

The redemptive sacrifice of Christ is unique, accomplished once for all; yet it is made present in the Eucharistic sacrifice of the Church. The same is true of the one priesthood of Christ; it is made present through the ministerial priesthood without diminishing the uniqueness of Christ's priesthood: "only Christ is the true priest, the others being only his ministers."

page 430, paragraph 1545

If Christ's sacrifice accomplished the redemption of mankind for those who will believe through faith, then why would Christ make himself present again in the Eucharistic sacrifice of the Catholic Church? By the very nature of the word *sacrifice,* the Catholic Church is offering something other than what Christ himself offered on the cross at Calvary, which was himself. Since the Catholic Church has decided to make this offering, what would be the purpose or intent behind that? You see, you cannot side step the Word of God on this issue. Hebrews 9:25–28 says,

> Not that He should offer Himself often as the high priest enters the most holy place every year with blood of another- He then would have had to suffer often since the foundation of the world; but now once at the end of the ages, He has appeared to put away sin by the sacrifice of Himself. And as it is appointed for men to die once, but after this the judgment, so Christ was offered once to bear the sins of many. To those who eagerly wait for Him He will appear a second time, apart form sin, for salvation.

I'm not really sure how the authors will get around these four verses in God's Word, as it pertains to the Eucharistic sacrifice. But, one thing is for certain; Christ is not offering himself often. He was offered once at the end of the ages and was offered once to bear the sins of many. So, I'm not really sure how the authors came to believe they are offering Christ in the Eucharistic sacrifice. Then, in Hebrews 10: 10, 12, 14 and 18, it says,

> By that will we have been sanctified through the offering of the body of Jesus Christ once for all.
>
> Hebrews 10: 10

> But this man, after He had offered one sacrifice for sins forever, sat down at the right hand of God.
>
> Hebrews 10: 12

> For by one offering he has perfected forever those who are being sanctified.
>
> Hebrews 10: 14

> Now where there is remission of these, there is no longer an offering for sin.
>
> Hebrews 10: 18

✝

It is the same priest, Christ Jesus, whose sacred person his minister truly represents. Now the minister, by reason of the sacerdotal consecration which he has received, is truly made like to the high priest and possesses the authority to act in the power and place of the person of Christ himself (virtute ac persona ipsius Christi). Christ is the source of all priesthood: the priest of the old law was a figure of Christ himself, and the priest of the new law acts in the person of Christ.

page 431, paragraph 1548

This paragraph has two major problems from a biblical prospective. First, we cannot and do not act in the person of Christ. There is no replacement theology at work in the world today. Christ is the same today, yesterday, and forever. The only thing any person born of the Spirit of God can do is be his representatives here on earth. Second Corinthians 5:20 says, "Therefore we are ambassadors for Christ, as though God were pleading through us; we implore you on Christ's behalf, be reconciled to God." Secondly, there is no new law in the Bible. We are now living within the new covenant, or the age of grace. Christ did not come and die on the cross to establish a new law, but to establish a new covenant with man directed by Father God. He died to do away with the law (first covenant). The Law was simply a means by which the LORD showed us that we could not keep it and were in need of his saving grace. All who will come to him during this time of grace may be saved through faith in his finished work at Calvary!

†

Through the ordained ministry, especially that of bishops and priests, the presence of Christ as head of the Church is made visible in the midst of the community of believers. In the beautiful expression of St. Ignatius of Antioch, the bishop is Typos Tou Patros: he is like the living image of God the Father.

page 431, paragraph 1549

Christ is made visible when people born of his Spirit allow his Spirit to work through them in their community. Being ordained by men has never been, and never will be, a stamp of approval from God, only men and women who will do the will of God as directed by the Holy Spirit. Furthermore, no man should be compared to or said to look like the living image of God. Men are sinful created beings, even on our best days. God the Father, Son, and Holy Spirit are sinless and are without beginning or end.

†

The sacrament of Holy Orders communicates a "sacred power" which is none other than that of Christ.

page 432, paragraph 1551

There is no such sacrament of "Holy Orders" in the Bible, and the only sacred power found is available to every man, woman, and child who calls on the Holy Spirit, the only power that abides in any believer.

✝

The ministerial priesthood has the task not only of representing Christ—head of the Church—before the assembly of the faithful, but also of acting in the name of the whole Church when presenting to God the prayer of the Church, and above all when offering the Eucharistic sacrifice.

page 432, paragraph 1552

The priest should be praying for the churches needs, but it is not his responsibility to present God with the prayer of the church. Each person within the body of Christ has direct access to the throne room of God and has the responsibility of praying for their needs and the needs of others. In so far as the offering of the Eucharistic sacrifice, there is no responsibility to bear because there is no more need of sacrifice for sin. Christ has already accomplished that on the cross! Psalm 51:16–17 says, "For you do not desire sacrifice, or else I would give it; you do not delight in burnt offering. The sacrifices of God are a broken spirit, a broken and a contrite heart. These, O God, you will not despise."

✝

The prayer and offering of the Church are inseparable from the prayer and offering of Christ, her head; it is always the case that Christ worships in and through his Church.

page 432, paragraph 1553

I believe this sentence would correctly read, "Christ is always worshiped in and through his church.

†

Let everyone revere the deacons as Jesus Christ, the bishop as the image of the Father, and the presbyters as the senate of God and the assembly of the apostles. For without them one cannot speak of the Church.page 433, *paragraph* 1554

Exodus 20: 4–5 says,

> You shall not make for yourself any carved image, or any likeness of anything that is in heaven above, or that is in the earth beneath, or that is in the water under the earth; you shall not bow down to them nor serve them. For I, the LORD your God, am a jealous God, visiting the iniquity of the fathers on the children to the third and forth generation of those who hate me.

Here again, it seems the authors will be found wanting when they will have to explain why they are in direct opposition to the commandments of God.

†

In our day, the lawful ordination of a bishop requires a special intervention of the bishop of Rome, because he is the supreme visible bond of the communion of the particulm Churches in the one Church and the guarantor of their freedom.

page 434, paragraph 1559

Christ is the guarantor of our freedom; no man or institution should be so bold or prideful to assume this title.

✝

Through that sacrament priests by the anointing of the Holy Spirit are signed with a special character and so are configured to Christ the priest in such a way that they are able to act in the person of Christ the head.

page 435, paragraph 1563

This must be like transubstantiation, where the priest is turning the bread and wine into the blood and body of Christ, except now they are able to act in the person of Christ. This theology may as well be called *replacement,* because these men are taking the free gifts of God and the Holy Spirit and saying they are now issued through them. Even to go so far as to say they are, "able to act in the person of Christ." Nowhere in the Bible do you find men or women proclaiming to be able to act in the person of Christ, but rather, men and women who were lead and filled with the Holy Spirit doing those things which the Spirit had instructed them to do.

✝

The spiritual gift they have received in ordination prepares them.

page 436, paragraph 1565

Spiritual gifts by its own name are gifts given by the spirit of God, not of men. First Corinthians 12: 4–11 says,

> Now there are diversities of gifts, but the same Spirit. There are differences of activities, but it is

> the same God who works all in all. But the manifestation of the Spirit is given to each one for the profit of all: for to one is given the word of wisdom through the Spirit, to another the word of wisdom through the Spirit, to another the word of knowledge through the same Spirit, to another gifts of healings by the same Spirit, to another the working of miracles, to another prophecy, to another discerning of spirits, to another the interpretation of tongues. But one and the same Spirit works all these things, distributing to each one individually as He wills.

✝

The sacrament of Holy Orders marks them with an imprint ("character"), which cannot be removed and which configures them to Christ, who made himself the "deacon" or servant of all.

page 437, paragraph 1570

You see, these men are being marked by men with an imprint which cannot be removed, and yet again, you see men of the Bible being marked by the seal of the Holy Spirit. Second Corinthians 1: 21–22 says, "Now He who establishes us with you in Christ and has anointed us is God, who also has sealed us and given us the Spirit in our hearts as a deposit." Ephesians 4:30 says, "And do not grieve the Holy Spirit of God, by whom you were sealed for the day of redemption."

✝

Called to consecrate themselves with undivided heart to the LORD *and to "the affairs of the* LORD.*" They give themselves entirely to God and to men. Celibacy is a sign of this new life to the service of which the Church's minister is consecrated; accepted with a joyous heart celibacy radiantly proclaims the reign of God.*

page 440, paragraph 1579

The idea behind celibacy is that it is a gift. If God has given you the spiritual gift to remain celibate, then it is better for you to serve him that way. Then, you will not have the concerns of a family to take care of. First Corinthians 7: 7–9 says,

> For I wish that all men were even as I myself. But each one has his own gift from God, one in this manner and another in that. But I say to the unmarried and to the widows. It is good for them if they remain even as I am; but if they cannot exercise self-control, let them marry. For it is better to marry than to burn with passion.

First Timonthy 3:2 says, "A bishop then must be blameless, the husband of one wife, temperate, sober minded, of good behavior, hospitable, able to teach." The problem becomes evident when you look at the authors' teachings on celibacy and you look at what the Word of God teaches. The bishops are allowed to be married according to the Word of God, and in the Catholic Church they are forbidden to marry.

†

In the Eastern Churches a different discipline has been in force for many centuries; while bishops are chosen solely from among celibates, married men can be ordained as deacons and priests. This practice has long been considered legitimate; these priests exercise a fruitful ministry within their communities. Moreover, priestly celibacy is held in great honor in the Eastern Churches and many priests have freely chosen it for the sake of the kingdom of God. In the east as in the west a man who already received the sacrament of Holy orders (can no longer marry).

page 440, paragraph 1580

The problem in this paragraph is two-fold. First, men should not choose to be celibate on their own for this is a gift from God, and second, marriage is not to be forbidden. Timothy 4:1–3 says,

> Now the Spirit expressly says that in the latter times some will depart from the faith, giving heed to deceiving spirits and doctrines of demons, speaking lies in hypocrisy, having their own conscience seared with a hot iron, forbidding to marry, and commanding to abstain from foods which God created to be received with thanksgiving by those who believe and know the truth.

†

Sacramentals derive from the baptismal priesthood: every baptized person is called to be a "blessing," and to bless.

page 464, paragraph 1669

You will find no mention of a priesthood after Christ died on the cross for our sins, let alone a baptismal priesthood. The only priesthood that remains after Christ's death and resurrection is the royal priesthood of believers in Christ. This priesthood is the people who are born again of the Spirit of God. First Peter 2: 9–10 says,

> But you are a chosen generation, a royal priesthood, a holy nation, His own special people, that you may proclaim the praises of Him who called you out of darkness into his marvelous light; who once were not a people but are now the people of God, who had not obtained mercy but now have obtained mercy.

Remember, Christ is our High Priest.

†

In a simple form, exorcism is performed at the celebration of baptism. The solemn exorcism, called "major exorcism," can be performed only by a priest and with the permission of the Bishop.

page 465, paragraph 1673

There can be no exorcism of a person except in and through the power of the Holy Spirit. The act of baptizing a person who is demon possessed would simply be cleaning up a demon-possessed person with some water. All authorities, demonic and otherwise, are under the power of the Holy Spirit, so when a person filled with the Holy Spirit commands a demonic spirit to leave, the demon or demons must obey. An example of this is found in Acts 8: 7–17.

For unclean spirits, crying with a loud voice, came out of many who were possessed; and many who were paralyzed and lame were healed. And there was great joy in that city. But there was a certain man called Simon, who previously practiced sorcery in the city and astonished the people of Samaria, claiming that he was someone great, to whom they all gave heed, from the least to the greatest, saying, "This man is the great power of God." And they heeded him because he had astonished them with his sorceries for a long time. But when they believed Philip as he preached the things concerning the kingdom of God and the name of Jesus Christ, both men and woman were baptized. Then Simon himself also believed; and when he was baptized he continued with Philip, and was amazed, seeing the miracles and signs which were done. When the Apostles who were at Jerusalem heard that Samaria had received the word of God, they sent Peter and John to them, who, when they had come down, prayed for them that they might receive the Holy Spirit. For as yet he had fallen upon none of them. They had only been baptized in the name of the LORD Jesus. Then they laid hands on them, and they received the Holy Spirit.

John 14:12 says, "Most assuredly, I say to you, he who believes in Me, the works that I do he will also; and greater works than these he will do, because I go to my Father." You see, the authors here again find themselves opposing the Word of God. Jesus said, "He who believes in Me, the works that I do he will do also." Notice, he does not say Catholic priests only will do these works.

✝

The Church who, as mother, has borne the Christian sacramentally in her womb during his earthly pilgrimage, accompanies him at his journey's end, in order to surrender him "into the Father's hand."

page 468, paragraph 1683

The church, who is the bride of Christ, is never referred to as a mother in the Bible. A Christian is not, and will not, be "borne sacramentally." The only way a Christian is born is by the Spirit of God. This whole mother concept sounds nice, but there simply is no biblical basis for it!

✝

The Eucharistic Sacrifice. When the celebration takes place in Church, the Eucharist is the heart of the Paschal reality of Christian death. In the Eucharist, the Church expresses her efficacious communion with the departed: offering to the Father in the Holy Spirit the sacrifice of the death and resurrection of Christ, she asks to purify his child of his sins and their consequences, and to admit him to the Paschal fullness of the table of the kingdom. It is by the Eucharist thus celebrated that the community of the faithful, especially the family of the deceased, learn to live in communion with the one who "has fallen asleep in the LORD," *by communicating in the body of Christ of which he is a living member and, then, by praying for him and with him.*

page 469, paragraph 1689

Here again, you find the authors offering a sacrifice that Christ himself could only offer once and for all. To suggest that these men are somehow benefiting you by this sacrifice would be cheapening or suggesting that what Christ already did is somehow not enough for our forgiveness of sins, and herein lies the problem; no one or anything is needed to aid us into the fullness of Christ. It is by our faith in his finished work on the cross that will sustain us in this life and carry us directly into his presence in the life to come! Either you believe the word of God, that the work is complete in Christ Jesus, or you are still trying to work your way toward God through the works of men's hands. Furthermore, there is no need to pray for a family member who has died. That family member is either in the presence of God or is in hell, and in either case, our prayers cannot change a person's place in eternity.

✝

By the sacraments of rebirth, Christians have become "children of God," "partakers of the divine nature."

page 471, paragraph 1692

By the Spirit of the living God and their faith in him, people have become "children of God" and "partakers of the divine nature."

†

Human beings make their own contribution to their interior growth; they make their whole sentient and spiritual lives into means of growth (article 6). With the help of grace they grow in virtue (article 7), avoid sin, and if they sin they entrust themselves as did the prodigal son to the mercy of our Father in heaven (article 8). In this way they attain to the perfection of charity.

page 474, paragraph 1700

Second Corinthians 3: 16–18 says,

> Nevertheless when one turns to the Lord, the evil is taken away. Now the Lord is the Spirit, and where the Spirit of the Lord is, there is liberty. But we all, with unveiled face, beholding as in a mirror the glory of the Lord, are being transformed into the same image form glory to glory, just as by the Spirit of the Lord."

It is only by the grace of God that we grow in our faith to begin with. Then, as we rely on his Spirit to change us, he is faithful and just to do so. I'm afraid if we rely on our own contributions to our interior growth, we will forever be coming up on the short end of the stick. Paul knew this well when he said,

> And not only they, but we also who have the first-fruits of the Spirit, even we ourselves groan within ourselves, eagerly waiting for the adoption, the redemption of our body. For we were saved in this hope; for why does one still hope for what he sees? But if we hope for what we do not see, then we eagerly wait for it with perseverance. Likewise the

> Spirit also helps in our weaknesses. For we do not know what we should pray for as we ought, but the Spirit himself makes intercession for us with groanings which cannot be uttered. Now He who searches the hearts knows what the mind of the Spirit is, because He makes intercession for the saints according to the will of God.
>
> Romans 8: 23–27

Paul had learned how weak he was in his own flesh and how strong he could be as he relied more and more on the spirit of God.

✝

With beatitude, man enters into the glory of Christ and into the joy of the trinitarian life.

page 479, paragraph 1721

This statement is extremely misleading. With beatitude, a person could just be having a good day mentally, but that will not get him or her entrance into the glory of Christ or a relationship with him. One can only enter into the glorious relationship with Christ through repentance and faith. You know, in some societies, pagan people can demonstrate beatitudes, but unless they repent of their sins and come to Christ through faith, they will die in their sins, even though they might have demonstrated beatitudes!

†

Conscience is a law of the mind; yet (Christians) would not grant that it is nothing more; I mean that it was not a dictate, nor conveyed the notion of responsibility, of duty, of a threat and a promise… [Conscience] is a messenger of him, who, both in nature and in grace, speaks to us behind a veil, and teaches and rules us by his representatives. Conscience is the aboriginal Vicar of Christ.

page 490, paragraph 1778

It sounds as though the conscience that the authors are speaking about is none other than the Holy Spirit, who dwells richly within every person born of the Spirit. But, if the authors are referring to conscience as the Holy Spirit, then the authors would be incorrect in saying he speaks to us from behind a veil and that he teaches and rules us by his representatives. Second Corinthians 3: 12–18 says,

> Therefore, since we have such hope, we use great boldness of speech unlike Moses, who put a veil over his face so that the children of Israel could not look steadily at the end of what was passing away. But their minds were hardened. For until this day the same veil remains uplifted in the reading of the Old Testament, because the veil lies on their heart. Nevertheless when one turns to the Lord, the veil is taken away. Now the Lord is the Spirit and where the Spirit of the Lord is, there is liberty. But, we all, with unveiled face, beholding as in a mirror the glory of the Lord, are being transformed into the same image from glory to glory, just as by the Spirit of the Lord.

John 14:26 says, "But the Helper, the Holy Spirit, whom the Father will send in my name, He will teach you all things, and bring to your remembrance." Second Timonthy 3: 15–17 says, "and that from childhood you have known the Holy Scriptures, which are able to make you wise for salvation through faith which is in Christ Jesus. All Scripture is given by inspiration of God, and is profitable for doctrine, for reproof, for correction, for instruction in righteousness, that the man of God may be completely thoroughly equipped for every good work.

Lastly, the Holy Spirit has no need of a vicar of Christ on earth! The Holy Spirit is still doing the same works he did in the apostles' lives and in men and women's lives today.

✝

The gift of faith remains in one who has not sinned against it. But "faith apart from works is dead": when it is deprived of hope and love, faith does not fully unite the believer to Christ and does not make him a living member of his body.

page 498, paragraph 1815

Faith is the only thing that fully unites the believer to Christ and makes him a living member of his body. Galatians 3: 24–28 says,

> Therefore the law was our tutor to bring us to Christ, that we might be justified by faith, but after faith has come, we are no longer under a tutor. For you are all sons of God through faith in Christ Jesus. For as many of you as were baptized into Christ have put on Christ. There is neither Jew nor Greek, there is neither male nor female; for you are all one in Christ Jesus.

Once again, you will find the only thing that will bring us into a right relationship with Christ is our faith. You can't add anything to Christ's finished work on the cross; either believe by faith or die in your sins.

✝

Service of and witness to the faith are necessary for salvation.

page 499, paragraph 1816

This statement is also contrary to the Word of God. The only thing necessary for salvation is our faith. Romans 10:9 says, "That if you confess with your mouth the LORD Jesus and believe in your heart that God has raised him from the dead, you will be saved." This verse is also consistent with what Jesus told the thief on the cross. All the thief had to do was believe that Jesus was the Son of God and ask him to forgive his sins, and Jesus said, "Today you will be with me in paradise."

✝

Christian hope takes up and fulfills the hope of the chosen people which has its origin and model in the hope of Abraham, who was blessed abundantly by the promises of God fulfilled in Isaac, and who was purified by the test of the sacrifice.

page 499, paragraph 1819

Abraham was found righteous by God, through his faith in who God is, not by a work or a test of the sacrifice. Genesis 15:6 says, "And he believed in the Lord, and He accounted it to him for righteousness." Abraham was blessed because he was found to be obedient in the offering of his son, Isaac. Genesis 22: 17–18 says,

> In blessing I will bless you, and in multiplying I will multiply your descendants as the stars of the heaven and as the sand which is on the seashore; and your descendants shall possess the gate of their enemies. In your seed all the nations of the earth shall be blessed, because you have obeyed My voice.

Our purity comes through our faith alone, and our blessings come as we are found being obedient to the voice and word of the Lord.

†

Charity upholds and purifies our human ability to love, and raises it to the supernatural perfection of divine love.

page 502, paragraph 1827

Charity means "an act or feeling of good will or affection." An act we do can never purify our human ability to love. But, the Holy Spirit can and does uphold and purifies our human ability to love and raises it to the supernatural perfection of divine love.

✝

"You shall call his name Jesus, for he will save his people from their sins." The same is true of the Eucharist, the sacrament of redemption.

page 504, paragraph 1846

Would this mean that if you took this sacrament of redemption that you would be saved by something you did? This supposed sacrament is not found in the Bible. The difference between the quote from Matthew and the quote here is that if anyone believed in Jesus as the Son of God, they would be saved from their sins. The same is true today; if anyone calls on the name of the LORD, they will be saved. He will not ask you if you also took the sacrament of redemption and believed he was the Son of God. His standard for redemption is and always will be belief in his Son, and you will not and cannot add anything to that!

✝

Venial sin does not deprive the sinner of sanctifying grace, friendship with God, charity and consequently eternal happiness

page 508, paragraph 1863

This statement has an apathetic approach to sin, and God is in no way, shape, or form apathetic toward any sin, small or great. Psalm 45:7 says, "You love righteousness and hate wickedness." Psalm 101: 4–8 says,

> A perverse heart shall depart from me; I will not know wickedness. Whoever secretly slanders his neighbor, Him I will destroy; the one who has a

> haughty look and a proud heart, Him I will not endure, My eyes shall be on the faithful of the land, that they may dwell with Me; He who walks in a perfect way, He shall serve me. He who works deceit shall not serve me. He who works deceit shall not dwell within my house; He who tells lies shall not continue in my presence. Early I will destroy all the wicked of the land, that I may cut of all the evildoers from the city of the LORD.

Proverbs 6:16–19 says,

> "These six things the LORD hates, yes, seven are an abomination to Him: a proud look, a lying tongue, hands that shed innocent blood, a heart that devises wicked plans, feet that are swift in running to evil, a false witness who speaks lies, and one who sows discord among brethren."

It's important to be very careful in how we think about all or any sin because God hates it all. We must guard our hearts and minds from the smallest of sin to the greatest. But, one thing is certain: sin always separates our fellowship with God, and for this reason we must be quick to repent of any and all sin.

†

Venial sin constitutes a moral disorder that is reparable by charity, which it allows to subsist in us.

page 511, paragraph 1875

Any sin is natural to our fleshly nature and is reparable by repenting of your sin to Jesus, who is faithful and just to forgive us. Will you trust in the works of the flesh or in the Spirit of the living God?

✝

Divine help comes to him in Christ through the law that guides him and the grace that sustains him.

page 526, paragraph 1949

Divine help comes to us in Christ through the Holy Spirit that guides us, and his grace sustains him.

✝

However, the law remains the first stage on the way to the kingdom.

page 530, paragraph 1963

The law works as a means by which we are able to see that we are not able to keep it and thus are in need of a savior who, by the power of the Holy Spirit, begins to transform us into the image of his Son. Romans 3:20 says, "Therefore by the deeds of the law no flesh will be justified in his sight, for by the law is the knowledge of sin." Galatians 3:21–26 says,

> Is the law then against the promises of God? Certainly not! For if there had been a law given which could have given life, truly righteousness would have been by the law. But the Scripture has confined all under sin, that the promise by faith in Jesus Christ might be given to those who believe. But before faith came, we were kept under guard by the law, kept for the faith which would after-

> ward be revealed. Therefore the law was our tutor to bring us to Christ, that we might be justified by faith. But after faith has come, we are no longer under a tutor. For you are all sons of God through faith in Christ Jesus.

†

The new law is called a law of love because it makes us act out of the love infused by the Holy Spirit, rather than from fear; a law of grace, because it confers the strength of grace to act, by means of faith and the sacraments; a law of freedom, because it sets us free from the ritual and juridical observances of the old law, inclines us to act spontaneously by the prompting of charity and, finally, lets us pass from the condition of servant who " does not know what his master is doing" to that of a friend of Christ—" for all that I have heard from the Father I have made known to you"—or even to the status of son and heir.

page 533, paragraph 1972

The problem with this paragraph is that the authors are suggesting a new law now exists—the sacraments—a law for those who are set free in Christ. It is true that Christ said, "For all that I have heard from My Father I have made know to you," and he makes no mention of the new law, the sacraments, a law of freedom.

✝

God does not want each person to keep all the counsels, but only those appropriate to the diversity of persons, times, opportunities, and strengths, as charity requires.

page 533, paragraph 1974

I'm not sure what counsels the authors are referring to, but God does want us to keep all of *his* counsel, which is found in the Word of God. Acts 20:27–28 says, "For I have not shunned to declare to you the whole counsel of God. Therefore take heed to yourselves and to all the flock, among which the Holy Spirit has made you overseers, to shepherd the church of God which He purchased with His own blood."

Deut 10:12 says,

> And now, Israel, what does the LORD your God require of you, but to fear the LORD your God, to walk in all his ways and to love him, to serve the LORD your God with all your heart and with all your soul, and to keep the commandments of the LORD and His statutes which I command you today for your good?

John 14: 23–24 says,

> Jesus answered and said to him, "If anyone loves Me, he will keep My word; and My Father will love Him, and we will come to him and make our home with him. He who does not love Me does not keep My words; and the word which you hear is not mine but the Father's who sent Me."

Jeremiah 23:22 says, "But if they had stood in My counsel, and had caused My people to hear My words, then they would have turned them for their evil way and from the evil of their doings."

Micah 4:12 says, "But they do not know the thoughts of the LORD, nor do they understand His counsel."

Revelation 3:18–22 says,

> I counsel you to buy from Me gold refined in the fire, that you may be clothed, that the shame of your nakedness may not be revealed; and anoint your eyes with eye salve, that you may see. As many as I love, I rebuke and chasten. Therefore be zealous and repent. Behold, I stand at the door and knock. If anyone hears My voice and opens the door, I will come in and dine with him, and he with Me. To him who overcomes I will grant to sit with Me on my throne, as I also overcame and sat down with My Father on His throne. He who has an ear, let him hear what the Spirit says to the churches.

†

The grace of the Holy Spirit has the power to justify us, that is, to cleanse us from our sins and to communicate to us "the righteousness of God through faith in Jesus Christ" and through Baptism.

page 535, paragraph 1987

This sentence is fine until the authors add, "and through Baptism," because our faith in Christ is the only thing that can cleanse us from our sins. Baptism, as stated earlier, is simply being obedient to Christ's commandment to be baptized after you have been saved by your faith.

†

Justification is at the same time the acceptance of God's righteousness through faith in Jesus Christ.

page 536, paragraph 1991

This sentence is true and needs nothing added to it.

†

Justification has been merited for us by the passion of Christ who offered himself on the cross as a living victim, holy and pleasing to God, and whose blood has become the instrument of atonement for the sins of all men. Justification is conferred in Baptism, the sacrament of faith. It conforms us to the righteousness of God, who makes us inwardly just by the power of his mercy. Its purpose is the glory of God and of Christ, and the gift of eternal life.

page 536, paragraph 1992

This paragraph is where the authors start adding to the means by which a person is justified. They say justification is conferred in baptism. The only problem is that you cannot trust in an act or work for our justification. For those who have been justified through faith in Jesus Christ, baptism represents a person who has died to his flesh and risen in newness of life with Christ!

✝

Our justification comes from the grace of God." Grace is favor, the free and undeserved help that God gives us to respond to His call to become children of God, adoptive sons, partakers of the divine nature and of eternal life.

page 538, paragraph 1996

This is a true statement.

✝

The grace of Christ is the gratuitous gift that God makes to us of his own life, infused by the Holy Spirit into our soul to heal it of sin and to sanctify it. It is the sanctifying or deifying grace received in Baptism. It is in us the source of the work of sanctification:

page 538, paragraph 1999

So, is grace, as stated in paragraph 1996, "the free and undeserved help that God gives us," or is it a source of work, in which case would be something other than grace? You see, it is either one or the other, but it can't be both.

✝

Since the initiative belongs to God in the order of grace, no one can merit the initial grace of forgiveness and justification, at the beginning of conversion. Moved by the Holy Spirit and by charity, we can then merit for ourselves and for others the grace and charity, and for the attainment of eternal life.

page 541, paragraph 2010

So, let me get this straight. No one can merit the initial grace necessary for justification, but moved by the Holy Spirit and our works, we can then merit for ourselves and for others the grace and works and for the attainment of eternal life. This does not make sense! The authors have changed the very meaning of grace. Grace is from God, not for men to delegate as they wish. This delegation is a misuse of power, power over which they (the Catholic Church) have no authority. The authors cannot dictate the covenant that Father God gave all men through his son Jesus Christ.

✝

The children of our Holy mother the Church rightly hope for the grace of final perseverance and the recompense of God their Father for the good works accomplished with his grace in communion with Jesus.

page 543, paragraph 2016

This sentence makes no sense. Are we children of our LORD Jesus Christ and heavenly Father, or are we children of a holy mother? As I stated earlier, neither the church nor anyone one else in the Bible is ever referred to as our holy mother.

✝

Justification has been merited for us by the passion of Christ. It is granted us through baptism.

page 544, paragraph 2020

Justification has been given to us by the grace of God and has nothing to do with a work on our part or anyone else.

✝

The grace of the Holy Spirit confers upon us the righteousness of God. Uniting us by faith and Baptism to the passion and resurrection of Christ, the Spirit makes us sharers in his life.

page 544, paragraph 2017

The problem with this paragraph is the second sentence where the authors add baptism to the equation.

✝

Justification has been merited for us by the passion of Christ. It is granted us through Baptism. It conforms us to the righteous of God, who justifies us. It has for its goal the glory of God and of Christ, and the gift of eternal life. It is the most excellent work of God's mercy.

page 544, paragraph 2020

It is granted us through the Holy Spirit, which conforms us to the righteousness of God, who justifies us. It has for its goal the glory of God and of Christ and the gift of eternal life. It is the most excellent work of God's mercy. Justification is granted to us through faith in Christ, not a work.

✝

It is in the Church, in communion with all the baptized, that the Christian fulfills his vocation. From the Church he receives the word of God containing the teachings of "the law of Christ." From the Church he learns the example of holiness and recognizes its model and source in the all holy Virgin Mary; he discerns it in the authentic witness of those who live it; he discovers it in the spiritual tradition and long history of the saints who have gone before him and whom the liturgy celebrates in the rhythms of sanctoral cycle.

page 545, paragraph 2030

It is in the church, in communion with the Holy Spirit, that the Christian fulfills his vocation. From the Bible, we receive the word of God containing the teachings of "the law of Christ." From the Holy Spirit he receives the grace that sustains him on the way. From Christ we learn the example of holiness. The problem with this paragraph is three-fold. First, the Christian would be relying on the Catholic Church for the receiving of the Word of God instead of opening it for themselves. Second, they would be relying on the Catholic Church instead of the Holy Spirit for grace. Last, how is the church looking to another created sinful human being instead of Christ for their source of holiness?

†

As does the whole of the Christian life, the moral life finds its source and summit in the Eucharistic sacrifice.

page 546, paragraph 2031

This paragraph would suggest that the Catholic Church's sacrifice found in the Eucharist would be of some great value to the believer. But, I would suggest that the whole of Christian life is found not in something any church can offer you, such as their own sacrifice. Rather, it is found in the sacrifice Christ performed once and for all. Furthermore, we find our summit in the Christian life when we are abiding in Christ's holy spirit and his Word. John 14:23–26 says,

> Jesus answered and said to him, "If anyone loves me, he will keep My word; and My Father will love him, and we will come to him and make our home with him. He who does not love Me does not keep My words; and the word which you hear is not mine but the Father's who sent me. These things I have spoken to you while being present with you. But the helper, the Holy Spirit, whom the Father will send in My name, He will teach you all things that I said to you."

John 15:4–11 says,

> Abide in Me, and I in you. As the branch cannot bear fruit of itself, unless it abides in the vine, neither can you, unless you abide in Me. I am the vine; you are the branches. He who abides in Me, and I in him, bears much fruit; for without Me you can do nothing. If anyone does not abide in Me, he is cast out as a branch and is withered; and

> they gather them and throw them into the fire, and they are burned. If you abide in Me, and My words abide in you, you will ask what you desire, and it shall be done for you. By this My Father is glorified, that you bear much fruit; so you will be my disciples. As the Father loved Me, I also have loved you; abide in My love. If you keep My commandments, you will abide in His love. These things I have spoken to you, and that your joy may be full.

✝

The Church, the "pillar and bulwark of the truth," has received this solemn command of Christ from the apostles to announce the saving truth. To the Church belongs the right always and everywhere to announce moral principles, including those pertaining to the social order, and to make judgments on any human affairs to the extent that they are required by the fundamental rights of the human person or the salvation of souls.

page 546, paragraph 2032

This paragraph could say, The Bible is the pillar and bulwark of the truth, received by the believers; they should announce the saving truth as Christ has commanded. The Bible announces moral principles, including those pertaining to the social order, and in the hands of believers. We have the ability to make judgments on any human affairs to the extent that they are required by the fundamental rights of the human person.

✝

The supreme degree of participation in the authority of Christ is ensured by the charism of infallibility. This infallibility extends as far as does the deposit of divine revelation; it also extends to all those elements of doctrine, including morals, without which the saving truths of the faith cannot be preserved, explained, or observed.

page 547, paragraph 2035

This supposed infallibility, assumed by the Catholic Church, needs to take a look at its own troubled past because it becomes very apparent that the popes of the past made some extremely flawed decisions. Insofar as doctrine is concerned, I believe they have made numerous errors, which I have cited. Finally, the only thing that will be found infallible in this life or the next will be the Father, the Son (Word), and the Holy Spirit.

✝

The authority of the magisterium extends also to the specific precepts of the natural law, because their observance, demanded by the creator, is necessary for salvation.

page 547, paragraph 2036

Here, you find an adding to the requirements necessary for salvation.

†

Ministers should be exercised in a spirit of fraternal service and dedication to the Church.

page 548, paragraph 2039

Ministries should be exercised in and through the power of the Holy Spirit, fueled by our dedication to Christ. As you search the Scriptures, you will never find Paul or the other apostles saying they went through the trials of their ministries because of their dedication to "the church," meaning a hierarchy of people. These men did the things they did out of their love for Christ and their concern for the souls of men and women.

†

Personal conscience and reason should not be set in opposition to the moral law or the magisterium of the Church.

page 548, paragraph 2039

Personal conscience and reason should not be set in opposition to the moral law or the magisterium of the Church, except when these things are in clear opposition to the Word of God!

✝

Thus a true filial spirit the Church can develop among Christians. It is the normal flowering of the baptismal grace which has begotten us in the womb of the Church and made us members of the body of Christ. In her motherly care the Church, grants us the mercy God which prevails over all sins and is especially at work in the sacrament of reconciliation. With a mother foresight, she also lavishes on us day after day in her liturgy the nourishment of the word and Eucharist of the LORD.

page 548, paragraph 2040

We have all been begotten in our mother's womb by God. Psalm 71:5–6 says,

> For You are my hope, O LORD God; You are my trust from my youth. By You I have been upheld from my birth; You are He who took me out of my mother's womb. My praise shall be continually of You.

Psalm 139:13–16 says,

> For You have formed my inward parts; You have covered me in my mother's womb. I will praise You, for I am fearfully and wonderfully made; marvelous are Your works, and that my very well. My frame was not hidden from You, when I was made in secret, and skillfully wrought in the lowest parts of the earth. Your eyes saw my substance, being yet unformed. And in your book they all were written, the days fashioned for me, when as yet there were none of them.

So, to suggest that we are children of our mother, the church, is simply incorrect. The church is the bride of Christ, and we are children of God.

✝

The second precept ("You shall confess your sins at least once a year.") ensures preparation for the Eucharist by the reception of the sacrament of reconciliation, which continues baptism's work of conversion and forgiveness.

page 549, paragraph 2042

The only reconciliation that takes place is when a person comes to the Lord by faith and repents of their sins. Furthermore, the last part of this sentence proves that baptism does not save a person from their sins, or else you would not need a sacrament of reconciliation to continue baptism's work of conversion.

✝

The forth precept ("you shall keep holy the holy days of obligation.") completes the Sunday observance by participation in the principal liturgical feasts which honor the mysteries of the Lord*, the Virgin Mary, and the saints.*

page 549, paragraph 2043

Christ has done away with the holy days of obligation; he came to fulfill the law, not to reinstate it. The Lord says whatever you do, do it as unto him with thanksgiving. The best example of this is found in Colossians 2:11–22 which says,

"In Him you were also circumcised with the circumcision made without hands, by putting off the body of the sins of the flesh, by putting off the body of the sins of the flesh, by circumcision of Christ, buried with Him in baptism in which you also were raised with Him through faith in the working of God, who raised Him from the dead. And you, being dead in your trespasses and the uncircumcision of your flesh, He has made alive together with Him, having forgiven you all trespasses, having wiped out the handwriting of requirements that was against us, which was contrary to us. And He has taken it out of the way, having nailed it to the cross. Having disarmed principalities and powers, He made a public spectacle of them, triumphing over them in it. Therefore let no one judge you in food or in drink, or regarding a festival or a new moon or sabbaths, which are a shadow of things to come, but the substance is of Christ. Let no one defraud you of your reward, taking delight in false humility and worship of angels, intruding into those things which he has not seen, vainly puffed up by his fleshly mind, and not holding fast to the Head, from whom all the body nourished and knit together by joints and ligaments, grows with the increase which is from God. Therefore, if you died with Christ from the basic principles of the world, why, as though living in the world, do you subject yourselves to regulations—'Do not touch, do not taste, do not handle,' which all concern things which perish with the using—according to the commandments and doctrines of men?"

The Lord is asking you this question, why when I have been crucified to set you free from this legalistic way of thinking would you be willing to subject yourself to this kind of bonded. Also, if you want to have a feast or festival have it and enjoy it as unto the Lord. But, don't have it as unto one of his created beings, like Mary and the saints listed in the Bible. This would only dishonor yourself and the name of Jesus Christ. Remember, none of them paid the penalty for your sin.

✝

The moral life is a spiritual worship. Christian activity finds its nourishment in the liturgy and the celebration of the sacraments.

page 550, paragraph 2047

Christian activity should find its nourishment in the Word, prayer, fasting, and fellowship.

✝

Voluntary doubt about the faith disregards or refuses to hold as true what God has revealed and the Church proposes for the belief.

page 562, paragraph 2088

Let's talk about what God has revealed. We know that God has given us his Word, which gives us everything we need that pertains to living the Christian life. Second, Timothy 3:16–17 says, "All scripture is given by inspiration of God, and is profitable for doctrine, for reproof, for correction, for instruction in righteousness, that the man of God may be complete, thoroughly equipped for every good work." You know, when I was growing up, I was taught that the gifts of the Holy Spirit died at Pentecost. But as I took the time to read God's Word, I found that this is not true at all. In fact, it was quite the opposite; God wants us to pray for the gifts of the Holy Spirit. I'm saying that unless you take the time to read God's Word for yourself, you have no way of knowing whether or not the doctrines your church is teaching you are true or not! So, voluntary doubt is a good thing, especially when you are relying on the Holy Spirit and God's Word to show you whether or not the doctrinal precepts you are being taught are true! This skepticism should not be sown in discontent or malice but should be the sincere hunger of the soul for righteousness and person of God. Jesus told us to seek: "But seek first his kingdom and his righteousness, and all these things will be given to you as well" (Matthew 6:32–33, NIV), and "But seek his kingdom, and these things will be given to you as well" (Luke 12:31, NIV).

†

Incredulity is the neglect of revealed truth or the willful refusal to assent to it. "Heresy is the obstinate post-baptismal denial of some truth which must be believed with divine and Catholic faith, or it is likewise an obstinate doubt concerning the same; apostasy is the total repudiation of the Christian faith; schism is the refusal of submission to the Roman pontiff or of communion with the members of the church subject to him."

page 562, paragraph 2089

From a biblical prospective, heresy would be teaching something that is not in accordance with God's Word or adding something to his Word. Once again, the Catholic faith, or any other faith, is not the standard by which we will be judged. So, the choice is yours: you can be found to be heretical by the Catholic standard or by God's standard: his Word. You must take a look into the Word of God and determine who you are created to please. Would God ask you to keep the commandments of the Catholic Church if they are in opposition to his Word? Certainly not!

> Jesus recalls the words of the prophet Hosea: "I desire mercy, and not sacrifice." The only perfect sacrifice is the one that Christ offered on the cross as a total offering to the Father's love and for our salvation. By uniting ourselves with his sacrifice we can make our lives a sacrifice to God.
>
> page 565, paragraph 2100

Psalm 51:16–17 says, "For You do not desire sacrifice or else I would give it; You do not delight in burnt offering. The sacrifices of God are a broken spirit. A broken and contrite heart- These, O God, You will not despise." So, why would you have a Eucharistic sacrifice? Since Christ's sacrifice is the only perfect sacrifice, by which we are saved by faith, shouldn't we embrace the sacrifice he made and lay aside any imperfect sacrifice we can offer? The Lord would desire us to embrace the cross with holy living and not embrace man-made idolatry.

†

Catholic teaching on the moral duty of individuals and societies toward the true religion and the one Church of Christ.

page 566, paragraph 2105

A true Christian religion would be one that places God's Word as the highest importance by which we are to live. Our lives and the one true church of Christ are those born of his Spirit, found abiding in his Word.

†

Nobody may be forced to act against his convictions, nor is anyone to be restrained from acting in accordance with his conscience in religious matters in private or in public, alone or in association with others, within due limits.

page 567, paragraph 2106

How can the authors make this statement? One only has to look at the history of the Catholic Church to see that they have acted quite contrary to this statement. Let's take a look at a few examples from *The New Foxe's Book of Martyrs* by John Foxe. Concerning papal persecutions and the inquisition, it says,

> Up to about the 12th century, most of the persecutions against true believers in Christ came from the pagan world, but now the church in Rome discarded the truths of the scriptures and the commandments of love and took up the sword against all who opposed the false doctrines and traditions that had increasingly become part of it since the time of Constantine. During that time the Roman

> church drifted away from the orthodox beliefs for which so many had been martyred. It began to lay aside holiness, piety, humility, charity, and compassion, and take upon itself pagan superstitions and doctrines that were materially, physically, and socially beneficial to its clergy and gave them total domination in all church matters. Any who disagreed with them or their doctrines were branded as heretics who must be brought into agreement with the Papal church by force if necessary, and if the heretics did not repent and swear allegiance to the pope and his prelates, they must be executed. They justified the horrors they committed by wresting old testament scriptures, and by appeal to Augustine, who had interpreted Luke 14:23 as endorsing the use of force against heretics: " then the master said to the servant, 'go out into the highways and hedges, and compel them to come in, that my house may be filled.'"

For several centuries the Papal church raged throughout the world like a hungry beast, slaughtering thousands of true believers in Christ and torturing and mutilating thousands more. It was the "dark age" of the church. The Waldenses in France were the first victims of the fury of the Papal persecution.

About a.d. 1000, when the light of the true Gospel had almost been put out by darkness and superstition, a few who plainly saw the great harm that was being done to the church became determined to show the light of the Gospel in its real purity, and to drive off the clouds that scheming priests had raised over it to blind the people and hide its true brightness. The effort began with a man named Berengarius, who boldly preached the holy gospel as plainly seen in the scriptures. Down through the years others took up the torch of truth and brought light to thousands, until by the year a.d. 1140 there were so many reformed believers that the Pope became alarmed and wrote many princes, that they should drive them out of their principalities. He also had many of his most educated officials write letters against them.

Persecution of the Waldenses: About 1173, Peter Waldo, or Valdes, a wealthy Lyon merchant, well known for his piety and learning, gave his goods to the poor and became a traveling preacher and strenuous opposer to Papal prosperity and oppression. Before long a large number of the reformed in France joined with him—they became know as the Waldenses. At first, Waldo sought Papal recognition, thinking that he could influence the church in Rome, but, instead, he was excommunicated for heresy in 1184.

Waldo and his followers then developed a separate church with its own ministers. They preached religious discipline and moral purity, spoke out against unworthy clergy and the abuse of the church, and rejected the taking of Human life under any circumstances. The Papal church, however, would not allow such heresy to be taught, and separation from Rome could not be tolerated, so in a.d. 1208 the pope authorized a crusade against the Waldenses and other reformed groups, especially the Albigenses.

In a.d. 1211, eighty of Waldo's followers were captured in the city of Strasbourg, tried by inquisitors appointed by the pope, and burned at the stake. Shortly thereafter, most of the Waldenses withdrew into the Alpine valleys in northern Italy to live. Waldo died in 1218, still preaching the true Gospel of Christ.

Work and Persecution of Martin Luther (1517–1546):

Martin Luther, the son of a Saxon miner, was born in Eisleben, Saxony, on November 10, 1483. The young Luther studied at Magdeburg and Eisenach and then entered the University of Erfurt. When he graduated in 1505, he began to study law at the urging of his father, but in July he abandoned his law studies, renounced the world, and entered the monastery of the Augustinian Hermits at Erfurt. He credited this sudden decision to having been caught in thunderstorm and knocked to the ground by a bolt of lighting—as he lay on the ground in fear, he realized that his temporal life had little value and only the eternal life of his soul was important.

In 1508, Luther was ordained at the monastery, and in 1509, was sent to the University of Wittenberg where he continued his studies and lectured in moral philosophy. In 1510, Luther visited Rome on business for his order and was shocked to find open corruption among leading church officials. In 1511, he received a doctorate in theology, and was appointed professor of Scripture at Wittenberg.

Although Luther was well acquainted with Roman Catholic scholastic theology, the seriousness with which he took his Christianity and the condition of his soul led him into a severe personal crisis. In the theology that he had been taught, he could not find the answer to his increasing concern as to whether it was possible to reconcile the demands of God's law with human inability to live up to that law. To find his answer he made the study of the Bible the center of his work, and in his studies concentrated on the epistles of the Apostle Paul, especially Paul's letter to the Romans. It was there that he found his answer.

In the death of Jesus Christ on the cross, God had

reconciled humanity to himself. Christ was now the sole mediator between God and man, and forgiveness of sin and salvation are affected by God's grace alone, and are received by faith. What was required, therefore, was not a person's strict adherence to the law or the fulfillment of religious obligations, but a response of faith that accepted what God had done in the finished work of Christ. As such faith matured, it would lead to obedience based not on fear of punishment, but on love.

As Luther continued in his studies, he found that Paul's doctrines were radically different than the traditional beliefs and teachings of the Roman church. This affected Luther's personal teachings, and they soon began increasingly to turn away from those beliefs and doctrines. Before long he was totally against Roman scholastic theology that emphasized man's role in his own salvation, and against many church practices that emphasized justification by good works. His new understanding of the true Gospel and the finished work of Christ soon led to a clash between him and church officials.

In 1517, Luther had his first direct confrontation with his church over the selling of indulgences. To raise money to build St. Peter's Basilica in Rome, Pope Leo X started selling indulgences to Roman Catholics. These promised partial remission of the amount of time that a person, either the buyer or a loved one, had to suffer in purgatory for their sins. Soon after, some of the more cunning clergy saw the sale of indulgences as a way to raise money for their local churches or themselves. Luther considered himself a good Roman priest, but strongly objected to this practice because it was unscriptural and degraded the forgiving grace of

God and the suffering and crucifixion of Jesus Christ. Luther and Pope Leo immediately clashed over this, but Pope Leo considered Luther's objections to be of little consequences because he had little regard for Luther. So on October 31, 1517, Luther nailed to the main door of the castle church in Wittenberg a list of 95 propositions or theses. Among other things they denied the right of the pope to forgive sins by the sale of indulgences. Almost immediately the list was widely circulated in Germany and caused a great controversy. (See Appendix B for a complete list of the 95 theses.)

On the church side, friars and clerics throughout the region began attacking Luther and his teachings through their sermons and writings. One of them said, "Luther is a heretic, and worthy to be persecuted with fire." He then burned some of Luther's writings and sermons as a symbolic burning of Luther.

Soon after, Maximillian, emperor of Germany, Charles V, Holy Roman emperor and king of Spain as Charles I, demanded that he silence Luther. Frederick did not move immediately, but consulted many educated men on the problem, including *Erasmus. Erasmus answered the duke by saying that Luther had two great faults: he would touch the clerics' bellies, and he would touch the clerics' bellies, and he would touch the pope's crown. More seriously, the theologian told the duke that Luther was right in his desire to correct errors in the church. He then added this affirmation: "The effect of Luther's doctrine is true."

Later that year, Erasmus wrote to the archbishop of Mentz. In his letter, he stated, "the world is burdened with men's institutions, and with the tyranny of begging friars. Once it was counted a heresy when a man opposed the gospels. But now he is a heretic who is not like the friars, and whatsoever they do not understand is heresy to them. To know Greek is heresy, or to speak more finely than they do, that is heresy."

On August 7, 1518, Hierome, bishop of Ascoli, issued a citation requiring Luther to appear at Rome. Duke Frederick and the University of Wittenberg wrote letters to the pope on Luther's behalf. They wrote a similar letter to the pope on Luther's behalf. They wrote a similar letter to Carolous Miltitius, the pope's chamberlain, a German-born believer whom they judged to be somewhat sympathetic to Luther. In their letters they requested that Luther be heard by Cardinal Cajetan in Augsburg instead of Rome. The pope responded by telling Cajetan to summon Luther before him in Augsburg and immediately bring him to Rome, by force if necessary.

In October 1518, Martin Luther went to Augsburg in response to the cardinal's order. He took several letters of days until a warrant of conduct could be obtained from the emperor Maximillian. Luther then appeared before Cardinal Cajetan, who demanded three things from him:

1. That he repent and revoke his errors;
2. That he not to revert back to those errors;
3. That he refrain from all things that might trouble the church.

When Martin Luther asked the cardinal what his specific errors were, the cardinal showed him a copy of remission of sins, stated that faith isn't necessary for a person who receives the sacrament, and that the pope was infallible in all matters of faith.

In his written reply, Luther said the pope was capable of error and was only to be obeyed so long as what he said agreed with the Scriptures, and that any faithful Christian has the right to disagree with him and to point out to him his errors from the Word of God; he also stated that no one is righteous and cannot be made so by works, and that anyone receiving the sacraments must have faith in the finished work of Christ. In every case, Luther quoted the appropriate Scriptures to confirm his words.

The cardinal, however, did not want to hear the Scriptures quoted to him in that manner. He ignored Luther's biblical arguments and responded with intellectual and traditional doctrines from his own head rather than from the Scriptures. He then told Luther to go away until he was ready to repent. Luther stayed in Augsburg for three days, and then sent a letter to the cardinal telling him that he would keep silent about the conditions and pardons offered to him if his enemies did the same. He also asked that all points of controversy be referred to the pope for his decision. He then waited another three days, but received no reply from the cardinal. Upon the advice of friends, he left Augsburg and returned to Wittenberg. Before he left, he sent an explanation to the cardinal and an appeal to the pope, which he had posted in public places before he left.

In response to Luther's appeal to him, the pope issued a new edict. He declared that indulgences were a part of the "holy Mother Church of Rome, the prince of all churches," and stated that popes are successors of Peter and, as such, they are vicars of Christ. He stated further that they have the power and authority to release from sin and dispense forgiveness, and to grant indulgences to both the living and the dead—those who remain in purgatory. This doctrine, he said, must be received by all the faithful followers of Christ, and warned Catholics that if they did not accept and practice these doctrines, they would suffer the pain of a great curse, including utter separation from the church.

Luther responded by appealing to the general council of the Roman Catholic Church, protesting this papal edict. When Pope Leo X learned of Luther's complaint to the general council, he sent his chamberlain, the German-born Carolus Miltitius, with a golden rose to be given to Duke Frederick. Miltitius also carried secret letters from the pope to other noblemen in the region. The letters solicited their support for the pope's cause and their rejection of the duke's support for Luther.

Before Miltitius reached Germany, however, Holy Roman Emperor Maximillian I died (January 1519). Two other prominent leaders immediately contended for the vacant throne: Francis 1, king of France; and Charles 1, king of Spain. By the end of August, Charles had been elected German king and Holy Roman emperor, as Charles V, in succession to Maximillian, who was his paternal grandfather.

During the summer of 1519, continued controversy swirled about Martin Luther and his teachings. A formal public debate took place at Leipsic, a city under the dominion of George, Duke of Saxony, one of Duke Frederick's uncles. The debate was between a friar named John Eckius and a doctor of Wittenberg named Andreas Carolostadt. Eckius had attacked certain teachings given by Luther, especially those related to papal pardons. Carolostadt, on the other hand, was strong in his defense of Luther. Duke George promised safe conduct to the participants and their audience. Martin Luther decided to attend the debate, not to take part in it, but simply to listen to what was said.

Despite his intentions to the contrary, Luther was compelled to dispute with Eckius. The particular issue under consideration was the authority of the pope. Luther took his familiar stance regarding decrees from the pope. He stated that unless the papal decrees are backed up by the Scriptures, they are invalid.

Eckius took the traditional line of the church by saying that popes are the successors of St. Peter and, as such, they have full spiritual authority over the church. They are, therefore, Christ's vicars on earth. He strongly stated that the bishop of Rome's authority is firmly grounded in God's law.

The debate continued for five days. Eckius was rude, defiant, and guileful in his approach. He wanted to deliver his adversary into the hands of the pope. He stated his reasons in the following manner: "Forasmuch as the church, being a civil body, cannot be without a head, therefore, as it stands with God's law that other civil regiments should not be destitute of their head, so is it a requirement of God's law that the pope should be the head of the universal Church of Christ."

Martin Luther countered this argument by saying that the Church has a head—Jesus Christ Himself. He stated that He is the only head of the church. "The Church," he said, "does not need any other head because it is a spiritual body, not a temporal one."

Eckius then quoted Jesus' words as recorded in Matthew's gospel, "thou art Peter, and upon this rock will I build my Church" (Matt. 16:18).

Luther explained that this verse is a confession of

faith, and that Peter represents the universal Church, not just himself. The rock is Jesus Christ and his Word, not Peter.

Endeavoring to find other Scriptures to support his argument, Eckius quoted Jesus' words from John's Gospel, "Feed my sheep" (John 21:16). He said that these words were spoken by the LORD to Peter alone.

Martin Luther pointed out that after Jesus spoke these words to Peter, equal authority was given to all the apostles, and Jesus commanded them to receive the Holy Ghost, and that the Master then went on to say, " whosoever sins ye remit, they are remitted" (John 20:23).

Looking for additional sources of authority to confirm his position, Eckius pointed to the rulings of the Council of Constance. He cited their adherence to the pope, who, according the council, is "to be supreme head of the church." He cited their adherence to the pope, who, according the council, is "to be supreme head of the church." He said that the general council could not err in such an important matter.

Luther said that certain judgments and the authority of the Council of Constance are to be esteemed, but that other matters related to the council are questionable in that some are simply the judgments of men. He said, "This is most certain, that no council has authority to make new articles of faith."

Reports of this debate, which had no specific conclusion, circulated widely throughout Europe. Eckius remained convinced of his position, while Luther held fast to his belief in justification by faith and that the Scriptures are the chief rule of faith and practice.

In 1520, Luther completed three books in which he declared his views. The first was the *Address to the*

Christian Nobility of the German Nation, in which he encouraged the German princes to take the reform of the church into their own hands. The second was *A Prelude Concerning the Babylonian Captivity of the Church,* in which he attacked the Roman church and its theology of sacraments. The third was *On the Freedom of a Christian Man,* in which he defined his position on justification and good works. The friars and doctors of Louvain and Cologne condemned Luther's books as heretical. Luther responded to the condemnation by charging the clergymen involved with being obstinate, violent, malicious, and impious. On June 15, 1520, Pope Leo X issued a bull, Exsurge Domine, that gave Luther 60 days to recant, but it had no effect upon him or his doctrines.

In his first book to the nobility of Germany, Luther contended against three main papist premises, which were:

1. No temporal or nonreligious magistrate has any power upon the *spirituality, but these have power over the other.
2. Where any place of Scripture, being in controversy, is to be decided, no man may expound the Scripture, or be judge thereof, but only the pope.
3. No man has authority to call a council except the pope.

He also addressed several other matters in the book: the pride of the pope is not to be permitted, too much money is sent from Germany to the pope, priests should be permitted to have wives, liberty ought not be restrained in eating meats, willful poverty and begging should be abolished, Emperor Sigismund should have stood with John Huss and Jerome, heretics should be convinced by God's Word and not by fire, the first teaching of children should be centered on the Gospel of Jesus Christ and not on the traditions of the Roman church. After Charles V was crowned king of Germany and Holy Roman Emperor at Aix-la-Chapelle, Pope Leo sent two cardinals to Duke Frederick. Their mission was to convince the duke to take action against Luther. The cardinals first attempted to win the duke's favor by praising his nobility, leadership, family heritage, and other virtues. Then they made two specific requests in the name of the pope-that he would have all of Luther's books burned, and that would either send Luther to Rome or have him executed.

The duke responded by saying that the pope's own chamberlain had said that Luther should remain in his domain so that he would not be able to influence Roman Catholics in other lands. He then requested that the cardinals ask the pope to give his permission for *learned theologians and doctors to examine Luther's writings and teachings to determine if he was a heretic. If he was found to be one and would not recant, then the duke would not protect him any longer, but he would until then.

Before the cardinals returned to Rome, they gathered as many of Luther's books as they could find and publicly burned them. When Luther heard about this, he gathered a multitude of students and faculty from the University of Wittenberg and held a public burning of the pope's decrees and the bull that was issued against him. This burning of the documents took place on December 10, 1520.

In January 1521, Pope Leo X condemned Luther

for heresy and issued a Bull of Excommunication, Decet Romanum Pontificem, against Luther and ordered Emperor Charles V to execute it. Instead, the emperor called a "diet," or council, at Worms, and in April 1521, summoned Luther to appear before him.

A private audience with the emperor and a few other dignitaries was scheduled in the Earl Palatine's palace. Luther was secretly escorted there, but his appearance before the emperor did not remain a secret for long. A large crowd descended upon the palace guards in an effort to behold the mysterious Luther. The palace guards were unable to hold them back, and many climbed into the galleries where they could see and hear the proceedings. Once when Luther attempted to speak, Ulrick of Pappenheim commanded him to keep silent until such time as he would be asked to speak.

The representative of the bishop of Treves opened the session by saying: "Martin Luther! The sacred and invincible imperial majesty has enjoined, by the consent of all the estates of the holy empire, that you should appear before the throne of our majesty to answer two main questions: Did you write the books which we have stacked in front of you? Will you recant and revoke them, or will you stand by what you have written?"

Luther answered, "I humbly beseech the imperial majesty to grant me liberty and leisure to meditate so that I may satisfy the interrogation made to me without detriment to the Word of God and peril of my own soul."

After the princes debated his request, Eckius, gave the emperor's decision: "The emperor's majesty, of his mere clemency, grants one day for you to meditate with regard to your answer. Tomorrow, at this same hour, you will give us your answer, not writing, but in your own voice."

The herald then escorted the reformer to his chambers, where Luther prayed and studied to ascertain God's will concerning the answer he should give.

A large crowd gathered to hear Luther's answer the next morning. Eckius said to Luther, "Answer now to the emperor's demand. Will you maintain all your books which you have acknowledged as yours, or will you revoke any part of them, and submit yourself to the authorities God has appointed over you?"

Martin Luther answered, "Considering the fact that our sovereign majesty and your honors require plain answer, this I say and profess as resolutely as I may, without doubting [uncertainty] or sophistication [possibly means a misleading argument], that if I am not convinced otherwise by testimonies of the Scriptures themselves—or I believe not the pope, neither his general councils that have erred many times and have been contrary to themselves—then my conscience is so bound and held captive by these Scriptures and the Word of God that I will not and may not revoke any manner of thing. It would be ungodly and unlawful for me to go against my own conscience. Hereupon I stand and rest. I don't have anything else to say. God have mercy upon me!"

After the princes conferred again, Eckius said to Luther, "The emperor's majesty requires a simple answer from you, either negative or affirmative, to this question: Do you intend to defend all your works as being Christian?"

As nightfall approached, the assembled dignitaries had not reached a final conclusion regarding Luther.

They left the proceedings and had Luther escorted back to his lodging. When the group reconvened, a letter from the emperor was read to the assembly. In effect, the letter stated that even though Luther was wrong in not recanting this position, the emperor would honor his promise to keep him safe. Luther could therefore return home. Before he left, however, Luther was told that he would have to return to the emperor's court in twenty-one days.

A fierce campaign raged against Luther during that time. Bills were posted against him, and throughout the empire the name of Luther was on the lips of all-clergy and laity alike. During the three-week reprieve, the emperor directed that a solemn writ of *outlawry be issued against Luther and all those who took his part, and that wherever Luther could be found he be arrested and all his books be seized and burned. Luther took refuge in the Wartbutg castle, where he lived in seclusion for eight months. During that time he translated the New Testament into German and wrote a number of pamphlets.

About this same time, King Henry VIII of England wrote against Luther. He reproved Luther for his position concerning papal pardons, and he defended the supremacy of the bishop of Rome. As a result of Henry's written support, the pope honored the king by giving to him and his successors the glorious title, "Defender of the Faith."

In November 1521, Pope Leo X was stricken with a fever and died on December 1. He was forty-seven. Many suspected that he had been poisoned. His successor was named Pope Adrian VI, a scholar who had been a schoolmaster of Emperor Charles. Adrian was a native German who was brought up in Louvain. He was an educated man whose lifestyle was moderate and gentle, unlike some of his predecessors.

Though Adrian was the first pope to respond to the Protestant Reformation by attempting to reform the Roman Catholic Church, he still saw Luther as an enemy of the church and the pope. Shortly after his appointment to the role of pontiff, the emperor called for another assembly of the German states to be held in Nuremberg in 1522. Adrian addressed a letter to the assembly in which he expressed his views regarding Martin Luther. The body of his epistle follows:

We hear that Martin Luther, a new raiser-up of old and damnable heresies, first after the fatherly sentence also of condemnation awarded against him, and lastly, after the imperial decree of our well-beloved son Charles V, elect emperor of the Romans and Catholic King of Spain, being divulged through the whole nation of Germany, yet has neither been by order restrained, nor of himself has refrained from his madness, but daily more and more ceases not to disturb and replenish the world with new books, fraught full of errors, heresies, arrogance, and sedition, and to infect the country of Germany, and other regions about, with this pestilence; and endeavors still to corrupt simple souls and manners of men with the poison of his morally evil tongue. And, worst of all, has for his supporters not the common sort only, but also diverse personages of the nobility who have begun also to invade the goods of priests contrary to the obedience which they owe to ecclesiastical and temporal persons, and now also at last have grown unto civil war and dissension among themselves.

Do you not consider, O princes and people of Germany, that these be but prefaces and preambles to those evils and mischiefs which Luther, with the sect of his Lutherans, do intend and purpose hereafter? Do you not see plainly, and perceive with your eyes, that this defending of the truth of the Gospel, first begun by the Lutherans to be pretended, is now manifest to be but an invention to spoil your goods, which they have long intended? Or do you think that these sons of iniquity do tend to any other thing than under the name of liberty to displace obedience and so to open a general license to every man to do what he pleases?

They who refuse to render due obedience to priests, bishops, and the high bishop of all, and who daily before your own faces make their plunder of church-goods and refrain their hands from the spoil of lay-men's goods? Do you think they will not pluck from you everything they can get their hands on?

This miserable calamity will at length have an effect upon you, your goods, your houses, wives, children, dominions, possessions, and those temples [churches] which you hallow and reverence, unless you provide a speedy remedy against the same.

Where, we require you, in virtue of that obedience which all Christians owe to God and blessed Saint Peter, and to his vicar here on earth, that you confer your helping hands to quench this public fire, and endeavor and study, as best you can, how to reduce the said Martin Luther, and all other deceivers of these disturbances and errors, to better conformity and trade both of life and faith. And if they who are infected shall refuse to hear your admonitions, make provisions so that the part that still sound is not corrupted by the same disease. When this morally evil canker cannot with supple and gently medicines be cured, more sharp salves must be proved, and fiery searings. The putrefied members must be cut off from the body, lest the sound parts also be infected.

In such a way God did cast down into hell the schismatical brethren Dathan and Abiram; and he that would not obey the authority of the priest, God commanded to be punished with. So Peter, prince of the apostles, *denounced sudden death. So the old and godly emperors commanded Jovinian and Priscillian as heretics to be beheaded.

In the way, Saint Jerome wished that Vigilant, as a heretic, be given to the destruction of his flesh so that his spirit might be saved in the day of the Lord. So also did our predecessors in the Council of Constance condemn John Huss and his fellow, Jerome, to death, and Huss now appears to revive in Luther. If you shall imitate the worthy acts and examples of these forefathers, we do not doubt but God's merciful clemency will relieve his church.

The princes of the empire responded to the pope's call for Luther's punishment with a letter of their own. Here is a paraphrase of the essence of their response:

We understand that his holiness is afflicted with great sorrow with regard to Luther and his sect. We also recognize that the souls who are influenced by him are in danger of eternal perdition. We share in your sorrow.

Many people in Germany hold views similar to Luther's, and this is why formal punishment of Luther has not taken place heretofore. This would lead to great upheaval, possibly even war, within the empire.

Unless these grievances among the general population can be reformed, there is no hope of harmony in this matter between the secular and the church.

Therefore, we recommend that the pope should,

with the emperor's consent, summon a Christian council at some convenient place in Germany as soon as possible. At this council people should be encouraged to speak freely.

We recommend that Duke Frederick would see to it that Luther and his followers not be permitted to write, set forth, or print anything else. And that all preachers in the duke's dominion be forbidden from preaching and of Luther's views.

Any ministers who do not comply with this directive should be punished. Any new books should be submitted to church authorities for approval before being sold.

Priests who marry or leave their authorities should be punished by established church officials.

Immediately thereafter, one of Luther's followers, Andreas Carolostadt of Wittenberg, stirred up the people to take actions that provoked the pontiff and his *prelates even more. Among other things, Carolostadt encouraged the people to throw down images and statues in Roman churches. In March 1522, Luther returned to Wittenberg to restore order against these enthusiastic *iconoclasts who were destroying altars, images, and crucifixes.

Luther's reforming work during subsequent years included the writing of the small and large catechisms, sermon books, more than a dozen hymns, over 100 volumes of tracts, treatises, biblical commentaries, thousands of letters, and the translation of the whole Bible into German.

With Philipp *Melanchthon and others, Luther organized the Evangelical churches in the German territories whose princes supported him. He abolished many traditional practices, including confession and private mass.

Luther was sixty-three years old when he died on February 18, 1546. Melanchthon described the reformer's final hours as follows:

Wednesday last past, February 17, Dr. Martin Luther sickened of his accustomed malady, to wit, of the oppression of *humors in the orifice or opening of his stomach. This sickness took him after supper, with which he vehemently contending, required withdrawal into a by-chamber, and there he rested on his bed two hours, all which time his pains increased. As Dr. Jonas was lying in his chamber, Luther awaked, and prayed him to rise, and to call up Ambrose, his children's schoolmaster, to make a fire in another chamber; into which, when he was newly entered, Albert, Earl of Mansfield, with his wife, and diverse others at that instant came into his chamber.

Finally, feeling his fatal hour approaching, before nine o'clock in the morning, on February 18, he commended himself to God with this devout prayer: "My heavenly Father, eternal and merciful God, you have manifested unto me Your dear Son, our Lord Jesus Christ. I have known Him, I love Him as my life, my health, and my redemption. The wicked have persecuted, maligned, and afflicted Him whom I love. Draw my soul to You."

A few moments passed and then Luther repeated a prayer of commendation three times: "I commend my spirit in your hands, you have redeemed me, O God of truth." He followed his prayer with the recitation of a favorite Scripture: "For God so loved the world, that he gave his only begotten Son, that whosoever believeth in him should not perish, but have everlasting life" (John 3:16). At the finish, he closed his eyes and opened them no more.

Luther's enemies rejoiced at his death, thinking perhaps that his work would die with him. But it did not, of course, for it was based on the truth of the Word of God. And like the Word, Luther's doctrines endured and spread the true Gospel of Jesus Christ throughout the world.

> In closing I would like to sum up what I believe are the main points in the text. First, I believe every believer must determine what their basis for truth is. According to God, his Word is the only standard by which truth is established. You have probably heard the saying, "If you don't stand for something, you will fall for anything." I also believe I have clearly shown were the traditions of the Catholic Church and the Word of God do not always agree. So, will we believe the truth of God's Word, or will we believe the lie? You see, we are living in times were the truth of God's Word is being questioned on every side. The Word of God depicts a day when God himself will send a delusion on the people because they did not receive the love of the truth. Second Thessalonians 2:9–14 says,

The coming of the lawless one is according to the working of Satan, with all power, signs, and lying wonders, and with all unrighteous deception among those who perish, because they did not receive the love of the truth, that they might be saved. And for this reason God will send them strong delusion, that they should believe the lie, that they all may be condemned who did not believe the truth but had pleasure in unrighteousness. But we are bound to give thanks to God always for you, brethren beloved by the LORD, because God from the beginning chose you for salvation through sanctification by the Spirit and belief in the truth, to which He called you by our gospel, for the obtaining of the glory of our LORD Jesus Christ.

> Secondly, I believe God always wants his children to find their sufficiency solely in him. But, just like the Hebrews in Moses' time, we often want to back into bondage. Many of the Hebrews liked the comforts of Egypt even though they knew God did not design them to be slaves under a false religious system and its ruler. So, if the Hebrews wanted to remain in Egypt after God had provided a way of escape, would they have received the same plaques and judgments? Revelation 18:4–8 says,

And I heard another voice from heaven saying, "Come out of her, my people, lest you share in her sins, and lest you receive of her plagues. For her sins have reached to heaven, and God has remembered her iniquities. Render to her just as she rendered to you, and repay her double according to her works; in the cup which she has mixed, mix for her double. "In the measure that she glorified herself and lived luxuriously, in the same measure give her torment and sorrow; for she says in her heart 'I sit as queen, and am no widow, and will not see sorrow.' "Therefore her plagues will come in one day-death and mourning and famine. And she will be utterly burned with fire, for strong is the LORD God who judges her."

Thus says the LORD in Revelation 3:18–22,

> I counsel you to buy from me gold refined in the fire, that you may be rich; and white garments, that you may be clothed, that the shame of your nakedness may not be revealed; and anoint your eyes with eye salve, that you may see. As many as I love, I rebuke and chasten. Therefore be zealous and repent. Behold, I stand at the door and knock. If anyone hears my voice and opens the door, I will come in to him and dine with him, and he with me. To him who overcomes I will grant to sit with Me on My throne, as I also overcame and sat down with my Father on his throne. He who has an ear, let him hear what the Spirit says to the churches.

Lastly, the authors have erred in their handling of the Word of God. Thus says the LORD, Jeremiah 8:8–9, "How can you say, 'We are wise, And the law of the LORD is with us'? Look, the false pen of the scribe certainly works falsehood. The wise men are ashamed. They are dismayed and taken. Behold, they have rejected the word of the LORD; So what wisdom do they have?"

Finally, God is calling all people throughout the world to worship him in spirit and in truth. He is not pleased when we are found trusting in false and idolatrous practices! He is calling all people to lay aside religious practices which have no biblical merit. Turn to the true and living God! He is the Alpha and Omega, the beginning and the end. He holds the keys of death and hell, and he longs for all his children, not just the Catholic Church's children, to abide in him and his word! Would you listen to the Spirit call? Revelation 2:14–17 says,

> But I have a few things against you, because you have there those who hold the doctrine of Balaam, who taught Balak to put a stumbling block before the children of Israel, to eat things sacrificed to idols, and to commit sexual immorality. Thus you also have those who hold those who hold the doctrine of the Nicolaitans, which things I hate. Repent, or else I will come unto thee quickly, and will fight against them with the sword of my mouth. He that hath an ear, let him hear what the Spirit says unto the churches. To him that overcomes will I give to eat of the hidden manna, and will give him a white stone, and in the stone a new name written, which no one knows except him who receives it.

J. Vernon McGee has this to say about the subject.

> The doctrine of the Nicolaitans, we have seen that the church in Ephesus hated it, but here in there were some who were holding that doctrine. Although we do not know exactly what the doctrine was, it probably was a Gnostic cult developed by Nicolaus which advocated license in matters of Christians conduct and apparently a return to religious rituals by the clergy, ignoring the priesthood of all believers. Christ says that he hates it! You see, Christ hates as well as loves. We had better be careful that we are not indulging in things that He hates.
>
> McGee Vol 5 pg 908–909

Index

†

No one can have God as Father who does not have the church as mother page 55, paragraph 181

Enter into communion with God page 60, paragraph 197

The revealed truth of the Holy Trinity page 74, paragraph 249

We are called to share in the life of the blessed Trinity page 79, paragraph 265

Is creation symbolic? page 98, paragraph 337

God is pure spirit page 105, paragraph 370

Is Mary truly "mother of God" page 139, paragraph 495

Was Mary a perpetual virgin? page 140, paragraph 499

Was Mary the most excellent fruit of redemption? page 142, paragraph 508

Was Mary all holly? page 208, paragraph 721

She was conceived without sin page 208, paragraph 722

Was Mary the most humble of creatures? page 208, paragraph 722

Mary or Jesus fulfills the Father's loving goodness page 208, paragraph 723

Does Mary bring men into communion with Christ? page 209, paragraph 725

Mary mother of the living page 209 paragraph 726

Is the sole church of Christ Catholic? page 234, paragraph 816

Is the Catholic church alone, our help for salvation? page 234, paragraph 816

Is the Catholic church the only church of God? page 235, paragraph 817

The church is one page 250, paragraph 866

Her holiness in the saints page 250, paragraph 867

The Catholic church administers the totality of the means of salvation page 250, paragraph 868

Mary mother of Christ, mother of the church page 273, paragraph 963

Immaculate virgin, queen over all things page274, paragraph 966

Jesus or Mary as advocate or helper? page 274, paragraph 969

Imperfectly purified page 291, paragraph 1030

Is purgatory the final purification? page 291, paragraph 1031

Prayers for the dead page 291, paragraph 1031

Were Job's son's purified by their father's sacrifice? page 291, paragraph 1031

Purification after death page 297, paragraph 1054

Sacraments of the new law page 315, paragraph 1114

Are sacraments necessary for salvation? page 319, paragraph 1129

He himself is the meaning of all these signs page 325, paragraph 1151–1152

Is holy baptism the gateway to life in the spirit page 342, paragraph 1213

Baptism, is sin buried in the water? page 342, paragraph 1216

Salvation by baptism page 343, paragraph 1219

Jesus, baptism and the Eucharist page 345, paragraph 1225

Is baptism a bath that purifies, justifies and sanctifies? page 345, paragraph 1227

Is becoming a Christian accomplished in stages? page 346, paragraph 1229

Baptism properly speaking or having been born again? page 348, paragraph 1239

Is Holy Communion the food of the new life? page 349, paragraph 1244

Baptism shortly after birth or after being born again? page 350, paragraph 1250

Is baptism the source of new life? page 351, paragraph 1254

Is baptism necessary for salvation? page 352, paragraph 1256

Does desire for baptism provide assurance of salvation? page 352, paragraph 1259

Children and baptism page 353, paragraph 1261

By baptism is all sin forgiven? page 353, paragraph 1263

Does baptism purify from all sin? page 354, paragraph 1265

Does baptism make us members of the body of Christ? page 354, paragraph 1267

By baptism do we share in the priesthood of Christ? page 355, paragraph 1268

Is baptism the foundation of communion among all Christians? page 355, paragraph 1271

Does baptism seal the Christian? page 356, paragraph 1272

Can baptism be repeated? page 356, paragraph 1272

Is baptism the seal of eternal life? page 356, paragraph 1274

Is Christian initiation accomplished by three sacraments? page 356, paragraph 1275

Is God dependant on baptism? page 357, paragraph 1277

Baptismal grace page 357, paragraph 1279

Baptism imprints page 357, paragraph 1280

Is baptism a grace? page 357, paragraph 1282

Are there sacraments of Christian initiation? page 358, paragraph 1285

Is the Holy Spirit dependant on a sacrament? page 367, paragraph 1316

Do we participate in the Lord's sacrifice? page 368, paragraph 1322

Is Christ consumed in the Eucharist? page 368, paragraph 1323

How is the church kept in being? page 369, paragraph 1325

Is the Eucharist the summary of our faith? page 369, paragraph 1327

Christ's sacrifice or the church's offering? page 370, paragraph 1330

How are we united to Christ? page 370, paragraph 1331

Will the Eucharistic sacrifice help the dead? page 382, paragraph 1371

Does the church and the world have a great need for Eucharistic worship? page 385, paragraph 1380

Is Holy Communion a remedy for sin? page 390, paragraph 1393

Does the Eucharist preserve us from future sin? page 390, paragraph 1395

Do priests aid Christ in Eucharistic sacrifice? page 394,paragraph 1410

Are Catholic priests the only ministers who should preside over Holy Communion? Page 394, paragraph 1411

Confession to sinful men or a holy God? page 397, paragraph 1424

Penance of the Christian page 400, paragraph 1434

Eucharist and penance remedy page 400, paragraph 1436

Only God forgives sins page 402, paragraph 1441

The office of binding and loosing page 402, paragraph 1444

Is the church in separable from reconciliation with God? page 403, paragraph 1445

God's order for reconciliation page 403, paragraph 1447

A sinner is healed page 404, paragraph 1448

Jesus is the source of all forgiveness page 404, paragraph 1449

Does contrition of charity remit sin page405, paragraph 1452

Imperfect contrition page 405, paragraph 1453

Is confession to a priest necessary? page 405, paragraph 1456

Confess serious sins at least once a year page 406, paragraph 1457

Confession of everyday faults page406, paragraph 1458

Do we have to make satisfaction for our sin? page 407, paragraph 1459

Do penances help configure us to Christ page 407, paragraph 1460

Does the sacrament of holy orders have power to forgive sin. page 408, paragraph 1461

Can priest absolve sin? page 408, paragraph 1463

Is the priest the sign? Page 409, paragraph 1465

Do we convert to Christ through penance and faith? page 410, paragraph 1470

Can indulgences be applied to the living or the dead? page 411, paragraph 1471

Can fervent charity attain complete purification? page 411, paragraph 1472

Should we strive by works to put off the "old man" page 411, paragraph 1473

Is God's grace sufficient? page 412, paragraph 1474

Can the church's treasury set free from sin page412, paragraph 1476

Church treasury, prayers and good works page 412, paragraph 1477

Formulas of absolution page 413, paragraph 1481

Confess to a priest page 416, paragraph 1493

Do indulgences aid souls in purgatory? page 417, paragraph 1498

Do we participate in the saving work of Jesus page 423, paragraph 1521

Does anointing of the sick complete us? page 424, paragraph 1523

Communion while dying? page 424, paragraph 1524

Holy orders and matrimony contribute to salvation page 426, paragraph 1534

A kingdom of priests page 428, paragraph 1539

Priesthood of Aaron page 428, paragraph 1541

Sacrifice of Christ unique, accomplished once for all page 430, paragraph 1545

Acting in the power and place of the person of Christ page 431, paragraph 1548

Are priests like the living image of God the Father? page 431, paragraph 1549

Holy orders communicates a "sacred power" page 432, paragraph 1551

Ministerial priesthood page 432, paragraph 1552

Does Christ worship? page 432, paragraph 1523

Deacons as Jesus Christ, the bishop as the image of the Father page 433, paragraph 1554

Bishop, guarantor of freedom page 434, paragraph 1559

Priests act in the person of Christ? page 435, paragraph 1563

Spiritual gifts received by men or God? page 436, paragraph 1565

Men marked by men or the Holy Spirit? page 437, paragraph 1570

Celibacy a sign or gift from God? page 440, paragraph 1579

Priestly celibacy page 440, paragraph 1580

Baptismal priesthood page 464, paragraph 1669

Major exorcism page 465, paragraph 1673

The church as mother page 468, paragraph 1683

Communion with the dead page 469, paragraph 1689

Sacraments of rebirth page 471, paragraph 1692

Interior growth page 474, paragraph 1700

Beatitude page 479, paragraph 1721

Conscience or holy Spirit unveiled page 490, paragraph 1778

Faith does not fully unite the believer to Christ page 498, paragraph 1815

Service of faith? page 499, paragraph 1816

Abraham was blessed page 499, paragraph 1819

Charity purifies page 502, paragraph 1827

Jesus and Eucharist the same page 504, paragraph 1846

Sin and grace page 508, paragraph 1863

Venial sin, reparable by charity page 511, paragraph 1875

Divine help page 526, paragraph 1949

The law and the kingdom page 530, paragraph 1963

New law page 533, paragraph 1972

God does not want us to keep all counsels page 533, paragraph 1974

The Holy Spirit has power to justify us page 535, paragraph 1987

Justification page 536, paragraph 1991

Justification by faith or works? page 536, paragraph 1992

Justification/ the grace of God page 538, paragraph 1996

Is grace a work? page 538, paragraph 1999

Can we merit grace for ourselves? page 541, paragraph 2010

Are children of a holy Father or mother? page 543, paragraph 2016.

Faith and baptism page 544, paragraph 2017

Justification through baptism page 544, paragraph 2020

Justification merited page 544, paragraph 2020

From the church we receive page 545, paragraph 2030

Summit in Eucharistic sacrifice page 546, paragraph 2031

The church "pillar and bulwark of truth" page 546, paragraph 2032

Charism of infallibility page 547, paragraph 2035

Authority of the magisterium page 547, paragraph 2036

Spirit of the fraternal service page 548, paragraph 2039

Opposition to thee magisterium of the church page 548, paragraph 2039

Womb of the church page 548, paragraph 2040

Confess sins at least once a year page 549, paragraph 2042

Holy days of obligation page 549, paragraph 2043

Christian activity and nourishment page 550, paragraph 2047

Voluntary doubt page 562, paragraph 2088

Heresy page 562, paragraph 2089

Perfect sacrifice page 565, paragraph 2100

Catholic/ true religion/ one church of Christ page 566, paragraph 2105

Nobody may be forced to act against his convictions within due limits page 567, paragraph 2106